Comfort

MOB

Comfort

MOB

FOOD THAT MAKES YOU FEEL GOOD

Photography by David Loftus

HODDER &
STOUGHTON

CONTENTS

KEY TO SYMBOLS

V · vegetarian
VG · vegan
GF · gluten-free
DF · dairy-free

Welcome to *Comfort MOB*. This is the book we've always wanted to write – a cookbook packed with one hundred feel-good recipes designed to satisfy your stomach *and* soothe your soul.

If there's anything we're known for at MOB Kitchen it's our hearty, warming recipes. The kinds of dishes that'll fill you up and warm you to your core. But this isn't just a book about carbs and cheese, it's about redefining comfort food.

In order to do that, we thought long and hard about what it is that makes a dish comforting. We realized that it's often about texture, heat and – perhaps most importantly – about the way that food makes you feel. Because comfort food isn't just an arrangement of flavours or ingredients that have been scientifically calculated to make you feel a certain way.

Comfort food is about coming home to the smell of your favourite meal after a bad day at work. It's a dish that reminds you of family. It's about that feeling of warmth and satisfaction you get when you're full of good cooking, but not too full for dessert. It's about sharing the food that you love with the people you love, and it's about grating carrot into your bolognese because that's how you like it. With that in mind, we decided that each recipe in this book needed to adhere to one (or more) of the characteristics overleaf.

- **SQUIDGY:** Oil-soaked focaccia, handmade ravioli, pork dumplings, harissa lamb-stuffed aubergines, halloumi and griddled peach burgers, and the ultimate chocolate brownie. Dishes that collapse lovingly under the slightest bit of pressure.

- **CRISPY/CRUNCHY:** One of our favourite textures and the best way to add excitement to a mundane recipe. Say hello to the crispest pork belly crackling, good old fish and chips, celeriac schnitzel, almond praline rice pudding and a fried mozzarella sarnie.

- **STICKY:** If you're a meat-eater and you hear the word 'sticky', you immediately know you're in for a good meal. The stickiest chicken wings, spicy braised short ribs, and Korean fire chicken. And vegans … we've got you covered with our sweet and sour cauliflower and Sriracha-glazed tofu.

- **HEARTY:** Proper stick-to-your-ribs recipes that deliver pure, unadulterated comfort. Beef brisket lasagne, orzo cacio e pepe, the ultimate cheeseburger, all the cheesy greens – the list goes on. The pudding section in the book is ridiculous …

- **SPICY:** There's nothing like a bit of spice to warm you up from the inside out. Some of our invigorating faves include a king prawn laksa, vegan mapo tofu, udon noodles with hot oil and our spicy chicken katsu.

- **NOURISHING:** To our minds, comfort food doesn't have to mean stodge. It also encompasses food that makes you feel fantastic, whether that's a fragrant chicken pho, a roasted broccoli Caesar, jok mu (Thai rice porridge), coconut fish curry or dal.

- **WARMING:** This is where our soups and stews come into their own. Miso onion soup with sesame Gruyère toasts, creamy corn chowder, fancy fish stew, and a smoky aubergine chilli are just the tip of the iceberg.

We wanted to fill this book with nostalgic recipes from our own childhoods as well as comforting dishes from around the world. So, we reached out to experts on a variety of different cuisines to get their contributions. We were able to try recipes we've never heard of before (like varenyky – chubby Ukrainian dumplings) and have included authentic versions of well-loved classics, like beef rendang, thanks to talented chefs like Lara Lee. We are so proud of these collaborations and believe that sharing recipes, and having conversations about where they come from, is the way forward.

As always, there are loads of veggie and vegan recipes and, wherever possible, we've stuck to as few ingredients as we can. There may be some ingredients you haven't heard of before, and while there are loads of budget-friendly options in the book, there are also some (like the whole-baked seabass on page 186) that require a slightly more lux set of ingredients. This means these recipes don't stick to our initial feed four for a tenner format, so we've included a budget hack for each recipe and hope that you'll identify with the desire to treat yourself every now and then.

Comfort MOB is not only about those classic recipes that can be made cheaply and easily, it's also about pushing the boat out for special occasions. That's why we've included optional recipes for homemade pasta, hollandaise, bread and pastry that'll really test your mettle. We'll guide you through every step and we've tested out all these recipes with actual home cooks, so we know that you can make them, too. See this as a chance to learn some new skills.

We can't wait to see all your re-creations at home because, honestly, this is our best book to date. And we're not just saying that because you're probably holding it in your hands and thinking about whether or not to buy it right now. We mean that from the bottom of our hearts (and our stomachs). We hope you love it as much as we do.

Ben and the whole MOB Team x

What is Comfort Food?

JUN TANAKA

My ultimate comfort food is one of the simplest recipes ever. It is tamago kake gohan – egg on rice. It's a Japanese dish that can be eaten at any time of the day. To make it, start with a bowl of steamed Japanese rice, crack an egg on top then season with soy sauce. Break the egg with a pair of chopsticks and whisk together ... that's it! It probably sounds a bit strange but it is delicious. The hot rice thickens the egg and whisking it with the soy sauce makes it lighter, almost fluffy. The best way to describe this dish is a light, savoury rice pudding.

LIZZIE MABBOTT

My ultimate comfort food dish is the one that evokes memories from childhood, a time and a place of security; for me, that takes the form of braised beef ho fun soup. Slippery rice noodles with the softest melting beef in a rich anise-scented gravy is exactly everything I turn to when I am feeling under the weather, or I need cheering up.

KARAN GOKANI

Comfort food for me is a big tub of Ben and Jerry's Chocolate Fudge Brownie on the couch after a long day at the restaurant.

ED SMITH

My comfort food is pretty diverse – textures and flavours are often gentle, brothy, creamy or savoury, although I also frequently retreat to spice and heat – but I guess a unifying theme is it tends to work best when I'm on the sofa, and the food's in a bowl and can be eaten with just a fork or spoon, maybe some chopsticks.

GIZZI ERSKINE

My favourite comfort currently is toad in the hole. It's a lazy roast. I make a vat of onion gravy, get some proper bangers, I make the best Yorkshire puddings and have it with mash, peas and English mustard. It's really the most honest, faultless and delicious recipe.

SABRINA GHAYOUR

Comfort food is about quick, simple, delicious meals that truly satisfy when you need it most.

ORE ODUBA

What does comfort food mean to me? A hearty meal and a guilt-free, full stomach! All shared with the people you love the most.

ORIGINAL FLAVA

Comfort food means family memories to us. Sitting down on the sofa watching a film with custard & rum cake.

LAP-FAI LEE

Comfort food for me is home cooked food you never tire of making and eating.

RUPY AUJLA

My ultimate comfort food dish is slow cooked oxtail ragu. Blend up the soffrito, use good red wine and let the herbs do the work.

OLIA HERCULES

When you return from school feeling down, hoping your mum would make that dish, and of course she is telepathic and makes exactly the thing, and your worries dissolve in the bowl of dumplings and the neurons get wired and fixed in a way that makes dough forever a reminder of unconditional love and protection.

JIMI FAMUREWA

Jacket potato heaped with tuna mayo and cheese, pounded yam with egusi soup, wobbling scoops of soft-boiled egg precariously balanced on toast; comfort food, to me, signifies those intensely personal dishes that – in a life necessarily governed by compromise – are about nothing but undiluted pleasure.

NIK SHARMA

Food is a powerful medium and so often we tie certain meals fondly to memories and experiences in our lives. It's these meals and the combination of their flavours that are so dear to me and just the mere thought of them kicks in the nostalgia.

MILLI TAYLOR

Comfort food for me is about texture and mouthfeel. It's about buttery mash, silky mac and cheese or the softly whipped cream on a banoffee pie. Full fat and full flavour.

LARA LEE

Comfort food has the power to restore. It transports us, to our childhood, to a special place, to a treasured memory deep within. It's a warm embrace from an old friend, a simple pleasure, a safe refuge. It grounds us, it lifts us up, it brings us home.

RAVNEET GILL

My ultimate comfort food is a fat slice of chocolate cake warmed up so the ganache melts, with loads of cold pouring cream. Every, single, time.

JOSÉ PIZARRO

For me, comfort food is reassuring, satisfying food. It's the type of food that makes people happy, conjuring memories of the best of times, and creating them too. It's really what I cook for us at home after working in the restaurants all day, and when we're catching up with friends. It's warm, welcoming, soul food.

THOMASINA MIERS

The best sort of comfort food is using familiar ingredients and often familiar recipes; for the comfort is in the memory of those family dishes eaten so many times around a table with the people you love; that fish pie; those waffles; that incredible leek quiche; they all have a delicious store of nostalgic thoughts and associations rooted in the pleasure of breaking bread with those closest to you.

JOHN CHANTARASAK

Comfort food is nostalgic, providing solace and joy. For me, anything rice based is comfort food, it's my carb of choice – fried rice, rice porridge, coconut sticky rice, it's all good honest comfort food.

FRANKIE STEW

My ultimate comfort food dish is mac and cheese hands down, there's something about it. Whether it's raining outside or the sun's shining, this dish always comforts me like no other. I have to be careful I don't eat too much of it though and end up ruining it for myself.

MALLIKA BASU

Comfort food is what I turn to for a taste of my childhood home and the reassurance that everything will be okay in the end.

TOM STRAKER

My ultimate comfort dish is lasagne, a meal that was a regular at home growing up, and that memory of something so hot and delicious on the weekend has remained with me throughout my life, and even more whilst being a chef. I am always yearning for comfort in food when I am at home and wanting to totally relax when not working, and lasagne delivers every time!

HARVEY GUNN

My ultimate comfort food dish is a ragù of veal, soffrito, white wine and chicken stock. Melded with butter to al dente mezze maniche and topped with pecorino Romano.

OLD-SCHOOL BANGERS

The classic comfort food dishes
we all know and love.

CHEDDAR & CHUTNEY SAUSAGE ROLLS

⏱ 1 HR 15 MINS + 15 MINS CHILLING · SERVES 4

Cheddar and onion chutney work wonders in this sausage roll – keeping the inside really lovely and moist (sorry) while the outside remains bronzed and flaky like an unreliable Greek Adonis.

BUDGET HACK: Use 2 teaspoons of mixed dried herbs rather than the fresh thyme.

6 PORK SAUSAGES (APPROX. 400G/14OZ)

100G (3½OZ) CHEDDAR CHEESE

A SMALL HANDFUL OF FRESH THYME

1 TBSP ENGLISH MUSTARD

4 TBSP RED ONION CHUTNEY

1 MEDIUM EGG

1 PACKET OF READY-ROLLED PUFF PASTRY (APPROX. 320G/11¼OZ)

A HANDFUL OF SESAME SEEDS

SALT AND BLACK PEPPER

01   Preheat your oven to 180°C/160°C fan/gas mark 4.

02   Squeeze the sausages out of their skins into a bowl.

03   Grate the cheese, strip off the thyme leaves and add to the sausage meat with the mustard. Season with salt and pepper, and mix to combine.

04   Warm the chutney slightly, in the microwave or a small saucepan, so it spreads more easily. Crack the egg into a small bowl and whisk.

05   Unravel the sheet of puff pastry and cut in half length-ways. Spread the red onion chutney over the top of each rectangle.

06   Divide the sausage mixture into two equal parts. Lay out the mixture along the length of each pastry strip in a cylindrical shape – you want there to be a 1cm (½in) border.

07   Brush the top of the sausage meat and borders with some of the beaten egg. Tightly roll the pastry over the sausage meat to encase it. Cut into 12 sausage rolls and chill in the fridge for 15 minutes.

08   Brush the remaining egg over the sausage rolls and sprinkle over the sesame seeds. Bake in the oven for 30 minutes until cooked through and a deep golden brown. Serve.

MOB'S CHICKEN KIEV

⏱ 1 HR 30 MINS + 30 MINS CHILLING · SERVES 4

We spent a long time perfecting our Kiev and the secret to its success is a double herb butter that delivers a killer one-two combo of tarragon and parsley. And when those two are in the ring together, the crowd can't help but get on their feet. Serve your chicken on a bed of our heavyweight bacon-y mash and you'll be out for the count, MOB.

BUDGET HACK: Use a larger bunch of parsley instead of the two herbs.

1 BUNCH OF FRESH TARRAGON
1 BUNCH OF FRESH PARSLEY
200G (7OZ) SALTED BUTTER
2 GARLIC CLOVES
8 RASHERS OF SMOKED BACON
4 LARGE POTATOES
4 SKINLESS CHICKEN BREASTS
100G (3½OZ) PLAIN FLOUR
3 MEDIUM EGGS
100G (3½OZ) PANKO BREADCRUMBS
OLIVE OIL
SALT AND BLACK PEPPER

01   Finely chop the tarragon and parsley. Add half to a large bowl along with 150g (5½oz) of the butter. Grate in the garlic cloves then season with salt and black pepper before mashing it all together.

02   Wrap your butter in cling film and mould into a cylinder shape. Place in the fridge for 30 minutes to firm up.

03   Get a large frying pan over a high heat. Chop up the bacon into small pieces, add to the pan and fry until crispy.

04   Peel and quarter the potatoes. Tip into a large saucepan of cold salted water and bring to the boil. Once boiling, cook for 15 minutes until tender (a knife should slide into them easily). Drain in a colander and tip them back into the pan. Add the remaining butter, chopped parsley and tarragon, salt, black pepper and a small drizzle of olive oil. Mash everything together. Once mashed, add your bacon and fold it through. Cover with a lid to keep warm and set aside.

05   Chicken time. Cut a slit into the thick side of each chicken breast. Work the knife and your index finger into the slit and make a hole to hold the herby butter. Ideally you want to keep the slit quite small so the butter doesn't flow out.

06   Take your butter out of the fridge and cut into small discs. Squeeze them into each of the chicken breasts.

07   Preheat your oven to 200°C/180°C fan/gas mark 6.

08   Get out three bowls. Add the flour into one. Crack the eggs into another one then whisk and season with salt and black pepper. Tip the breadcrumbs into the third bowl. Dip each chicken breast in the flour, then the whisked eggs and finally the breadcrumbs.

09 Get the same frying pan over a high heat. Drizzle in a good splash of oil. Add the chicken breasts to the pan and cook for 4 minutes on each side, until the breadcrumbs are golden.

10 Remove the chicken from the frying pan and add to a baking sheet. Place in the oven for 14 minutes until cooked through.

11 Divide the bacon mash between four plates and top with the chicken kievs. Tuck in and enjoy!

ROASTED TOMATO & PEPPER SOUP WITH CHILLI CHEESE TOASTIES

V · ⏱ 45 MINS · SERVES 4

A big upgrade on your standard soup and sarnie situation. Tomatoes and peppers are roasted with garlic and thyme to give them extra depth of flavour before being whizzed up and served with our supreme chilli jam and cheddar toasties. Use cheap white bread here for ultimate crust-to-ooze ratio.

MAKE IT VEGAN: Use dairy-free cheese and butter for the toasties.

BUDGET HACK: Use ½ tsp of dried oregano instead of the fresh thyme.

2 RED ONIONS

4 RED PEPPERS (WE LIKE THE POINTED PEPPERS)

800G (1LB 12OZ) CHERRY TOMATOES ON THE VINE

1 GARLIC BULB

A HANDFUL OF FRESH THYME

3–4 TBSP CHILLI JAM

8 SLICES OF SOFT WHITE BREAD

250G (9OZ) EXTRA-MATURE CHEDDAR CHEESE

750ML (1¼ PINTS) VEGETABLE STOCK

A LARGE KNOB OF BUTTER

OLIVE OIL

SALT AND BLACK PEPPER

YOU WILL ALSO NEED A STICK BLENDER.

01   Preheat your oven to 220°C/200°C fan/gas mark 7.

02   Peel and cut the red onions into wedges. Deseed the peppers and cut into quarters. Take the cherry tomatoes off their vine. Tip everything onto your largest baking tray. Nestle in the garlic then drizzle over a good glug of olive oil. Scatter over most of the thyme and season generously with salt and black pepper. Roast in the oven for 30–35 minutes until the tomatoes have begun to burst and the veg is soft and beginning to char.

03   While the veg is roasting, prep your toasties. Spread the chilli jam over four slices of bread then grate the Cheddar cheese directly over each one. Top with the remaining bread slices.

04   Remove the thyme and garlic from the roasted veg then tip into a large saucepan. Squeeze the garlic out of its skin by pressing a knife down on it and add to the pan. Pour in the vegetable stock then blitz the soup until smooth using a stick blender. Season to taste with salt and black pepper. Keep warm over a low heat.

05   Get a large non-stick frying pan over a high heat. Add half the butter and let it melt. Once melted, fry two of the toasties for 1 minute on each side until golden, squashing them down with a fish slice as they cook for ultimate crispiness. Transfer to a plate and repeat.

06   Slice the toasties in half. Ladle the soup into four bowls, drizzle with olive oil and scatter over a few thyme leaves. Serve with the toasties for dunking.

PALE ALE FISH & CHIPS WITH QUICK TARTARE SAUCE

⏱ 1 HR 20 MINS · SERVES 4

We couldn't write a book on comfort food and not include a recipe
for fish and chips. We've perfected the lightest, crispiest batter using
fridge-cold pale ale and baking powder. Our chip hack? Deep frying
frozen oven chips — an absolute game changer.

BUDGET HACK: Use either cornichons or capers in the tartare sauce, doubling the amount.

8 TBSP MAYONNAISE

A HANDFUL OF PARSLEY

1 BANANA SHALLOT

6 CORNICHONS

1 TBSP CAPERS

1 TBSP MALT VINEGAR, PLUS A SPLASH, TO SERVE

1 LITRE (1¾ PINTS) VEGETABLE OIL (FOR FRYING)

1 KG (2LB 4OZ) OVEN CHIPS

200G (7OZ) PLAIN FLOUR, PLUS EXTRA FOR DUSTING

2 HEAPED TSP BAKING POWDER

330ML (11¼FL OZ) VERY COLD PALE ALE (OR LAGER)

4 THICK BONELESS SKINLESS WHITE FISH FILLETS (WE LIKE HAKE OR HADDOCK)

SALT AND BLACK PEPPER

CONDIMENTS OF YOUR CHOICE, TO SERVE

YOU WILL ALSO NEED KITCHEN PAPER.

01   Tartare sauce time. Squirt the mayonnaise into a bowl. Finely chop the parsley, shallot, cornichons and capers. Scrape everything into the mayonnaise. Pour in the vinegar, stir together and season with salt and black pepper. Set aside.

02   Get a large deep frying pan over a medium heat. Pour the vegetable oil into it, you want it to come no higher than two-thirds up the pan. Preheat the oven to 120°C/100°C fan/gas mark ½.

03   Heat the oil until 180°C/350°F or use a piece of bread to test the temperature. Drop it into the oil and if it browns in 20 seconds it is ready. Any quicker and the oil is too hot, any longer then it needs to be heated for longer.

04   Once the oil is ready, fry the oven chips in small batches for 5 minutes at a time until nice and golden. Remove with a slotted spoon and drain on kitchen paper. Transfer to a large baking tray and sprinkle with salt. Once all the chips are ready, put in the oven to keep warm.

05   Turn the heat down to low under the oil pan while you make the batter. Measure the flour, baking powder and 1 teaspoon of salt into a large bowl. Pour in the cold pale ale, whisking to create a thick batter.

06   Reheat the oil to 180°C/350°F or do the bread test. Pat the fish dry with kitchen paper. One at a time, dip a fillet into the batter, coating it completely then carefully drop into the oil. Fry for 3–4 minutes, turning halfway, until crisp and deeply golden. Remove with a slotted spoon and drain on kitchen paper. Transfer to a baking sheet and sprinkle with salt. Repeat with the remaining fish.

07 Keep the fried fish warm in the oven along with the chips. If you have any leftover batter, drop into the pan and fry for 1–2 minutes (hello scraps).

08 Divide the fish and chips between four plates and drizzle over some vinegar. Serve with the tartare sauce and plenty of condiments for people to help themselves.

ULTIMATE SPAG BOLLY

⏱ 2 HRS 15 MINS · SERVES 4

We know you love this one from the website, so we had to include it in here, too. The key to the ultimate Bolognese is, believe it or not, milk. A generous glug of the stuff tenderizes the meat and evens out the acidity of the tomatoes. Don't knock it till you've tried it.

BUDGET HACK: Make double the amount of sauce and freeze. Use in a lasagne, on a jacket potato or pimped up with spice and kidney beans for a chilli.

200G (7OZ) DICED PANCETTA
2 ONIONS
2 CARROTS
3 CELERY STICKS
3 FAT GARLIC CLOVES
750G (1LB 10OZ) BEEF MINCE
1 LARGE GLASS OF RED WINE
   (250ML/9FL OZ)
400ML (14FL OZ) BEEF STOCK
400ML (14FL OZ) WHOLE MILK
1 × 400G (14OZ) TIN OF PLUM
   TOMATOES
4 BAY LEAVES
500G (1LB 2OZ) SPAGHETTI
OLIVE OIL
SALT AND BLACK PEPPER
PARMESAN CHEESE, TO SERVE

01 Get a large saucepan over a medium heat and drizzle in some olive oil. Tip in the pancetta and fry until crisp, stirring occasionally.

02 Meanwhile, finely chop the onions, carrot, celery and garlic. Add to the pan along with a further drizzle of olive oil and fry for 8–10 minutes until soft.

03 Turn up the heat to high and tip in the beef mince. Use the back of your spoon to break the mince up and fry until brown.

04 Pour in the red wine. Once it has bubbled away by half, pour in the stock and milk followed by the plum tomatoes. Season well with black pepper and add the bay leaves. Bring to the boil, then reduce the heat to a low simmer, cover and cook for 1½ hours.

05 Check it every 20 minutes or so and give it a good stir. If it is catching on the pan, just add a splash of water.

06 After 1½ hours, remove the lid. Season to taste, remove from the heat and leave with the lid off for 15 minutes. The sauce is even better made the day before and then reheated.

07 In this time, get your spaghetti on. Cook in a large pan of boiling salted water for 1 minute less than the packet instructions say. Drain in a colander when ready.

08 Toss your spaghetti through the bolognese, then pile it into four bowls. Serve with lots of Parmesan grated over the top and tuck in!

FRENCH ONION MAC & CHEESE

V · 🕐 2 HRS · SERVES 4

What happens when an unstoppable force meets an immovable object?
The same thing that happens when French onion soup meets mac &
cheese: glorious mayhem. The crispy caramelized onion and Gruyère
topping on this dish is absolutely ridiculous, MOB. How could we not put
this world-beating little number in the book?

VEGGIE: Check the labels of the cheese if cooking veggie and find alternatives if needed.

BUDGET HACK: Just use 400g (14oz) Cheddar cheese instead of both cheeses.

3 LARGE ONIONS
100G (3½OZ) BUTTER
1 LARGE GLASS OF WHITE WINE
   (250ML/9FL OZ)
SMALL BUNCH OF FRESH THYME
450G (1LB) MACARONI
4 TBSP PLAIN FLOUR
800ML (28FL OZ) WHOLE MILK
200G (7OZ) EXTRA-MATURE
   CHEDDAR CHEESE
200G (7OZ) GRUYÈRE CHEESE
1 HEAPED TSP DIJON MUSTARD
100G (3½OZ) BREADCRUMBS
SALT AND BLACK PEPPER

01   Thinly slice the onions. Get a large frying pan over a medium heat. Add a third of the butter and wait until it's melted. Add the onions with a good pinch of salt. Leave to fry for 30 minutes, stirring occasionally, until the onions have completely softened and caramelized.

02   Once the onions are cooked, pour in the white wine and add a handful of the thyme, stripping the leaves from the stalks into the pan. Simmer until the white wine has reduced by half then take the pan off the heat. The onions can be prepared in advance and kept in the fridge.

03   Cook the macaroni in a large pan of boiling salted water for 2 minutes less than the packet instructions say to then drain in a sieve.

04   Meanwhile, make the cheese sauce. Get a large ovenproof frying pan over a medium heat. Add the remaining butter and melt. Tip in the flour and whisk to combine – this is your roux. Whisking constantly, slowly pour all of the cold milk into the flour mixture, a little at a time, to get a smooth sauce. Bubble the sauce for 5 minutes until thickened.

05   Grate in all the Cheddar cheese and half the Gruyère cheese. Once the cheese has melted, take the sauce off the heat, add the Dijon mustard and season with salt and black pepper.

06   Preheat your grill to high.

07   Tip the cooked macaroni and caramelized onions into the cheese sauce, reserving a tablespoon of the onions. Give everything a good mix and then top with the remaining onions and Gruyère cheese, and the breadcrumbs. Scatter over a handful more thyme leaves.

08   Slide under the hot grill until bubbling and golden brown. Serve at the table out of the pan.

ROASTED GARLIC CHICKEN PIE

⏱ 2 HRS · SERVES 4

If you're looking for a hearty, winter-warmer of a dish, this MOB classic
is for you. Break through the golden puff pastry to reach a deeply
savoury filling, flavoured with fresh herbs and laced with roast garlic.

BUDGET HACK: Use 2 teaspoons of dried mixed herbs instead of the fresh rosemary and thyme.

4 GARLIC BULBS

1KG (2LB 4OZ) SKINLESS BONELESS CHICKEN THIGHS

1 ONION

20G (¾OZ) BUTTER

1 FRESH ROSEMARY SPRIG

1 FRESH THYME SPRIG

200G (7OZ) DICED PANCETTA

40G (1½OZ) PLAIN FLOUR

500ML (17FL OZ) CHICKEN STOCK

200ML (7FL OZ) WHOLE MILK

1 SHEET OF PUFF PASTRY → FREEZE THE REMAINING PASTRY TO BE USED ANOTHER TIME

1 MEDIUM EGG

OLIVE OIL

SALT AND BLACK PEPPER

MASH AND/OR SAUTÉED GREENS, TO SERVE (OPTIONAL)

YOU WILL ALSO NEED BAKING PAPER, BAKING BEANS OR UNCOOKED RICE/ PULSES.

01   Preheat your oven to 190°C/170°C fan/gas mark 5.

02   Wrap the bulbs of garlic in baking paper, then place on a baking tray and roast for 45 minutes. Set aside until cool enough to handle. Squeeze the garlic out of its skin by pressing a knife down on it. Discard the skins, saving the caramelized flesh until later.

03   Chop your chicken into 5cm (2in) pieces and slice the onion.

04   Get a large frying pan over a high heat. Drizzle in some olive oil then tip in half of the chicken thigh chunks. Season with salt and black pepper, fry for 5 minutes until the chunks are nice and golden. Remove from the pan, then repeat with the remaining chicken and remove from the pan.

05   Turn down the heat to medium and melt the butter into the pan. Tip in the onions along with the rosemary and thyme sprigs. Cook for about 6 minutes until totally soft. Add the diced pancetta and turn up the heat. Fry until crispy and the onions are caramelized.

06   Add the flour and cook out for 2 minutes until it starts to smell biscuity, then gradually pour in the stock in small increments, whisking all the while to ensure you have a smooth sauce. Once your stock has been incorporated, do the same with the milk. Bring to a boil, then simmer for 2 minutes until the sauce has thickened.

07   Add the chicken and roasted garlic to the pan along with some salt and black pepper, and stir to combine. Simmer for 2 minutes.

08   Pour your filling into a pie dish. Roll out the pastry sheet to a 2mm (¹⁄₁₆in) thickness and top the pie. Beat the egg and brush this over the top of the pastry. Place the pie dish onto a baking sheet in the oven and bake for 25–30 minutes until golden. Serve at the table by itself, or alongside some mash and sautéed greens.

PROPER TARTIFLETTE

GF · ⏱ 50 MINS · SERVES 4

What could be more comforting than a dish that was created in the French Alps and designed to sustain residents through the freezing cold winter? Not much, to be honest. Crisp bacon, soft onion, tender potatoes and plenty of cheese make up the delicious bulk of this hearty dish. Make sure to source out Reblochon cheese – it's the only one that will do.

BUDGET HACK: This one is good as it is.

1KG (2LB 4OZ) CHARLOTTE OR DESIREE
    POTATOES → A WAXY POTATO IS
    BEST FOR THIS CLASSIC FRENCH
    DISH
2 ONIONS
250G (9OZ) SMOKED BACON LARDONS
1 GARLIC CLOVE
1 LARGE GLASS OF WHITE WINE
    (250ML/9FL OZ)
240G (8½OZ) REBLOCHON CHEESE
4 TBSP CRÈME FRAÎCHE
OLIVE OIL
SALT AND BLACK PEPPER
PICKLES (WE LIKE CORNICHONS AND
    PICKLED ONIONS), TO SERVE
GREEN SALAD, TO SERVE

01 Keeping the skin on, cut the potatoes into smallish cubes. Tip into a pan of cold salted water and bring to the boil. Once boiling, cook for 8–10 minutes until tender (a knife should slide into them easily). Drain in a colander and leave to cool.

02 Preheat your oven to 200°C/180°C fan/gas mark 6. Thinly slice the onions.

03 Get a large frying pan over a medium–high heat. Drizzle in a splash of olive oil and add the onions and bacon lardons. Smash the garlic clove with the back of a knife and add to the pan. Fry until the bacon is crisp and the onions are golden. Remove the garlic clove and pour in the white wine. Stir until nearly all bubbled away then take the pan off the heat.

04 Rub the garlic clove around the inside of a medium baking dish, then discard. Thickly slice the cheese.

05 Layer the potatoes, bacon, onions and cheese into the dish, keeping some cheese back for the topping. Spoon over the crème fraîche, season everything well with salt and black pepper then top with the remaining cheese.

06 Bake in the oven for 30 minutes until the cheese is melted and everything is bubbling and golden. For extra ooze, heat your grill to high and slide the dish under the hot grill for a couple of minutes until browned. Serve at the table for people to help themselves with pickles and a green salad.

AUBERGINE & CAULIFLOWER KORMA

VG, GF, DF · ⏱ 1 HR · SERVES 4

If you thought vegan food couldn't be rich and indulgent then this is the
dish to change your mind. We've given the classic creamy korma a kick
with green chilli blitzed into the curry paste.

BUDGET HACK: Replace
the flaked almonds with 2
tablespoons more of desiccated
coconut in the curry paste and
serve simply with coriander
scattered on top.

1 TBSP CUMIN SEEDS

1 TBSP CORIANDER SEEDS

THUMB-SIZED PIECE OF FRESH GINGER

1–2 GREEN CHILLIES (DEPENDING ON
   HOW SPICY YOU LIKE IT)

1 SMALL BUNCH OF FRESH CORIANDER

3 GARLIC CLOVES

1 TBSP GARAM MASALA

1 TSP TURMERIC

2 TBSP TOMATO PURÉE

2 TBSP DESICCATED COCONUT

4 TBSP FLAKED ALMONDS

1 AUBERGINE

1 CAULIFLOWER

2 × 400ML (14FL OZ) TINS OF COCONUT
   MILK

1 LIME, QUARTERED

VEGETABLE OIL

SALT AND BLACK PEPPER

RICE, TO SERVE

01   Toast the cumin and coriander seeds in a dry frying pan until
smelling great. Set aside.

02   Peel the ginger and roughly chop along with the chilli. Separate
the coriander stalks from the leaves. Put the garlic, ginger, chilli and
coriander stalks into a food processor along with the toasted seeds,
garam masala, turmeric, tomato purée, desiccated coconut and 2
tablespoons of flaked almonds. Pour in 2 tablespoons of vegetable oil
and a good splash of water. Blitz to a smooth curry paste, adding a little
more water if you need it.

03   Chop the aubergine and cauliflower into medium-sized chunks,
making sure to slice up all the cauliflower leaves and stalks as well
(they're the best bits!).

04   Get a large frying pan over a high heat. Drizzle in a good splash of
vegetable oil. Season the aubergine and cauliflower with salt and black
pepper. Chuck half into the pan and fry for around 5 minutes, stirring
occasionally, until the veg is just starting to colour. Tip into a bowl and
repeat with the remaining veg.

05   Put the frying pan back over a medium heat. Drizzle in a splash
more oil then spoon in the curry paste. Cook, stirring for 2–3 minutes,
until everything smells unreal then pour in the coconut milk. Stir to bring
the sauce together then add the veg back into the pan.

06   Bring the curry to a boil, reduce the heat and put a lid on. Simmer
for 15 minutes until the veg is tender, giving you time to cook some rice.

07   Roughly chop the coriander leaves. Season to taste then divide
between four bowls with a lime wedge in each then scatter over the
coriander leaves and remaining flaked almonds. Serve with the rice.

ULTIMATE JACKET POTATO WITH PORKY BEANS

GF · ⏱ 1 HR 40 MINS · SERVES 4

If you can imagine what a jacket potato, cheese and beans that's been given a sexy and tasteful *Queer Eye* makeover would look like – this is it. We slow-cook our pancetta and chorizo beans alongside the potato for the richest, most comforting meal imaginable.

GLUTEN-FREE: Check the labels of the chorizo and brown sauce if cooking gluten-free and find an alternative if needed.

BUDGET HACK: Use just chorizo or pancetta in the beans.

4 BAKING POTATOES
225G (8OZ) CHORIZO RING (WE LIKE USING SPICY HERE)
160G (5¾OZ) DICED PANCETTA
1 ONION
2 CARROTS
2 CELERY STICKS
3 FAT GARLIC CLOVES
3 FRESH ROSEMARY SPRIGS
4 BAY LEAVES
2 TSP SMOKED PAPRIKA
1 × 400G (14OZ) TIN OF PLUM TOMATOES
2 × 400G (14OZ) TINS OF WHITE BEANS (WE LIKE CANNELLINI OR HARICOT)
4 TBSP BROWN SAUCE
100G (3½OZ) EXTRA-MATURE CHEDDAR CHEESE
OLIVE OIL
SALT AND BLACK PEPPER

01   Preheat your oven to 180°C/160°C fan/gas mark 4.

02   Prick the potatoes all over with a knife then put onto a baking tray. Drizzle with olive oil and season generously with salt and black pepper. Roast in the oven for 1½ hours.

03   Bean time. Peel and slice the chorizo. Get an ovenproof pan or casserole pot over a medium heat and drizzle a little oil in. Chuck in the chorizo and pancetta. Fry, stirring occasionally, until the pancetta is crisp.

04   Meanwhile, roughly chop the onion, carrots and celery. Scrape into the pan and cook for 5 minutes, stirring occasionally, while you peel and finely chop the garlic.

05   Add the garlic to the pan, cook for 1 minute then chuck in the rosemary, bay and smoked paprika. Give everything a good stir, then tip in the tomatoes and beans along with their liquid. Squirt in the brown sauce and season with salt and black pepper.

06   Bring the beans to the boil, put a lid on the pan and shove into the oven alongside the potatoes for the remaining cooking time.

07   Get the jacket potatoes out the oven and place each one onto a plate. Cut open and drizzle in some olive oil. Season the beans to taste, removing the bay and rosemary, then pile on top of the potatoes. Grate over the Cheddar to serve.

BEEF BOURGUIGNON PIE

⏱ 3 HRS 30 MINS · SERVES 4

A slow-braised beef and red wine casserole,
topped with crispy, buttery, cheese straws. The most intensely
savoury filling that will rock your world.

BUDGET HACK: Forget about the cheese straws and top the pie with a simple puff pastry lid instead.

12 SMALL SHALLOTS
1KG (2LB 4OZ) BEEF SHIN
250G (9OZ) SMOKED BACON LARDONS
4 CARROTS
3 FAT GARLIC CLOVES
2 TBSP PLAIN FLOUR
2 TBSP TOMATO PURÉE
A HANDFUL OF FRESH THYME
4 BAY LEAVES
1 BOTTLE OF RED WINE
1 BEEF STOCK CUBE
1 PACKET OF READY ROLLED PUFF
    PASTRY (APPROX. 320G/11¼OZ)
50G (1¾OZ) COMTÉ OR EXTRA MATURE
    CHEDDAR CHEESE
A BIG PINCH OF CAYENNE PEPPER
300G (10½OZ) BUTTON MUSHROOMS
OLIVE OIL
SALT AND BLACK PEPPER
PEAS, TO SERVE

YOU WILL ALSO NEED A ROLLING PIN.

01   Preheat your oven to 170°C/150°C fan/gas mark 3.

02   Peel the shallots, keeping them whole if you can. Cut the beef into large chunks and season generously with salt and black pepper.

03   Get a large shallow ovenproof saucepan or casserole over a high heat. Drizzle a good splash of olive oil into the pan. Add the meat and fry, in batches if needed, until evenly browned. Set aside on a plate.

04   Lower the heat to medium and tip in the bacon lardons and shallots. Fry, stirring occasionally, until the bacon is crisp.

05   Meanwhile, cut the carrots into large chunks. Finely chop the garlic cloves. Scrape both into the pan and cook for 1 minute. Stir in the flour, cook for 1 minute more then squeeze in the tomato purée. Add the thyme and bay leaves and give everything a good mix.

06   Tip the beef and any juices back into the pan. Pour in the wine and crumble in the stock cube. Bring the stew to a boil then take off the heat. Put a lid on the pan and cook in the oven for 2–2½ hours until the meat is tender. It should fall apart when prodded with two forks.

07   Beef in the oven, it's pastry time. Unravel the sheet of puff pastry so that one of the shorter sides is towards you. Grate the cheese over the bottom half of the pastry, sprinkle over the cayenne pepper then fold the top half over the cheese topped pastry. Roll the two gently together with a rolling pin so that the pastry sticks to the cheese.

08   Cut into 12 strips. Twizzle each strip with your finger to create a twist. On a baking tray weave the cheese twists together to create a rough lattice pattern that's the same size as your beef pot. Put into the fridge to chill.

09 Once the meat is done, take the lid off the pan. Halve the mushrooms and chuck them in. Season the sauce to taste with salt and black pepper. Turn the oven up to 200°C/180°C fan/gas mark 6.

10 Get the cheese twists on their tray into the oven. Put the beef underneath. Cook for 15 minutes until the twists are puffed up and golden. Remove them and the beef from the oven. Arrange the lattice of pastry on top of the beef then return to the oven for a further 5 minutes so that the bottom of the pastry soaks up some of the tasty meat sauce. We like to serve this with peas. The ultimate pie.

CHORIZO TOAD IN THE HOLE WITH HOT-SAUCE GRAVY & MUSTARDY GREENS

🕐 1 HR 15 MINS · SERVES 4

A MOB take on the British classic. We've used chorizo sausages, hot sauce, and mustardy greens in lieu of more traditional ingredients. The key to getting the perfect rise on your Yorkshire is working quickly to pour the batter into the hot oil and not opening the oven door once it's cooking. We know it's tempting, but leave it shut.

BUDGET HACK: Use whatever mustard and hot sauce you have in your kitchen already.

3 LARGE EGGS

100G (3½OZ) PLAIN FLOUR PLUS 1 TBSP

200ML (7FL OZ) WHOLE MILK

8 COOKING CHORIZO SAUSAGES

1 ONION

400ML (14FL OZ) CHICKEN STOCK

½–1 TBSP HOT SAUCE (WE LIKE FRANK'S)

1 LARGE SPRING OR SAVOY CABBAGE

3 FAT GARLIC CLOVES

2 TSP MUSTARD (WE LIKE FRENCH'S)

A BIG SPLASH OF WHITE WINE OR APPLE CIDER VINEGAR

VEGETABLE OIL

SALT AND BLACK PEPPER

01 Preheat your oven to 230°C/210°C fan/gas mark 8.

02 Yorkshire pudding time. Crack the eggs into a large bowl. Add 100g (3½oz) of flour, the milk and 2 tablespoons of water. Whisk well to create a smooth batter then season generously with salt and black pepper.

03 Pour 3 tablespoons of veg oil into a medium high-sided roasting tin or baking dish. Add the chorizo sausages and roast in the oven for 5 minutes.

04 Get the tray out of the oven. Working as quickly as possible without burning yourself, evenly space the chorizo sausages around the tray then pour in your batter. Return to the oven for 20–25 minutes until puffed up and golden.

05 Gravy and greens time. For the gravy, finely chop the onion. Get a small saucepan over a medium heat and drizzle in a splash of oil. Scrape in the onion and fry until just golden. Add 1 tablespoon of flour and cook for 1–2 minutes, stirring continuously, then pour in the chicken stock. Bring the gravy to the boil, reduce the heat and simmer until thickened. Stir in the hot sauce to taste. Keep warm over a low heat.

06 For the greens, thinly slice the cabbage and garlic cloves. Get a large frying pan over a medium heat. Drizzle in a splash of oil and tip in the cabbage and garlic. Give everything a good mix and pour in 100ml (3½fl oz) of water – this will help the greens steam as they fry. Cook for 4–5 minutes until wilted. Stir through the mustard and season with salt, black pepper and a splash of vinegar to taste.

07 Serve the toad in the hole at the table for people to help themselves alongside the gravy and greens.

STEAK WITH PEPPERCORN SAUCE & HASSELBACK PARMESAN POTATOES

GF · ① 1 HR 10 MINS · SERVES 4

Presenting: our platonic ideal of the pub classic, steak and chips.
The peppercorn sauce is special – heaps of black pepper, a shallot,
some brandy, and double cream. Then, you've got the spuds. Roasted
with a layer of parm until deeply golden with crisp and lacy edges
of molten cheese, these are the Hasselbacks of your dreams.

GLUTEN-FREE: Check the labels of the stock if you're cooking gluten-free and find an alternative if needed.

BUDGET HACK: Use a lesser-known cut of steak such as a bavette.

1KG (2LB 4OZ) NEW POTATOES
50G (1¾OZ) PARMESAN CHEESE
1 TBSP BLACK PEPPERCORNS
1 BANANA SHALLOT
2 FAT GARLIC CLOVES
4 SIRLOIN STEAKS
100ML (3½FL OZ) BRANDY
250ML (9FL OZ) BEEF STOCK → USE THE
    BEST QUALITY YOU CAN GET
100ML (3½FL OZ) DOUBLE CREAM
OLIVE OIL
SALT AND BLACK PEPPER
BLANCHED GREEN BEANS, TO SERVE
    (OPTIONAL)

01   Preheat your oven to 220°C/200°C fan/gas mark 7.

02   Hasselback time. Put a potato onto a wooden spoon. Holding it still, cut slices down it's length; this stops you from accidentally slicing all the way through the potato. Repeat with all the potatoes.

03   Lay the potatoes, sliced-side up on a large baking tray. Drizzle with a good glug of olive oil and season with salt and black pepper. Roast in the oven for 40 minutes.

04   When the potatoes have a few minutes to go, finely grate the Parmesan cheese onto a chopping board. Crack the black pepper into a small bowl, set aside.

05   Reduce the oven to 200°C/180°C fan/gas mark 6. Scatter the Parmesan over the potatoes, getting into all of the cracks, then roast for a further 15 minutes whilst you cook the steaks.

06   Get your largest frying pan over a high heat. Wait until it is searing hot, this will take a couple of minutes.

07   Meanwhile, finely chop the shallot and smash the garlic in its skin with the back of a knife. Season the steaks generously with salt and black pepper. Drizzle some olive oil into the hot frying pan. Add the steaks and garlic and fry the steaks for 2–2½ minutes on each side. Put the steaks on a plate to rest.

08   Sauce time. Put the pan back over a medium heat, pour in a splash more oil, add the shallot and fry, stirring occasionally until golden. Pour in the brandy, use your spoon to scrape any crusty steak bits off the

bottom of the pan. Once the brandy has reduced by half, pour in the stock. Bubble away for a minute or so then add the cream along with the cracked black pepper. Cook, stirring for 1–2 minutes, until the sauce has thickened slightly. Remove from the heat. Get rid of the garlic cloves and season with salt and black pepper. Pour the resting steak juices into the sauce and mix to combine.

09 Divide the crispy cheesy hasselbacks between four plates. Serve with a steak and the peppercorn sauce poured over. If you want some added health, serve with some blanched green beans.

THE BEST FISH STEW

GF · ⏱ 1 HR 15 MINS · SERVES 4

This recipe is inspired by one of our favourite restaurant dishes: a French bouillabaisse. Specifically, the one from The Cow in London. We've simplified it, but kept the sauce rich.

GLUTEN-FREE: If serving with bread, choose a gluten-free alternative.

BUDGET HACK: Instead of the prawns use 500g (1lb 2oz) of clams along with the mussels instead.

1 ONION

1 FENNEL BULB

3 GARLIC CLOVES

1 TBSP FENNEL SEEDS

2 TSP SMOKED PAPRIKA

2 TBSP TOMATO PURÉE

1 LARGE GLASS OF WHITE WINE
   (250ML/9FL OZ)

400G (14OZ) TIN OF PLUM TOMATOES

400ML (14FL OZ) FISH STOCK

150G (5½OZ) GREEK YOGHURT

1 LEMON

500G (1LB 2OZ) MUSSELS

4 BONELESS SKINLESS WHITE FISH
   FILLETS (WE LIKE HAKE, SEABASS
   OR COD)

8 SHELL-ON FRESH RAW KING PRAWNS

A HANDFUL OF BASIL LEAVES

OLIVE OIL

SALT

CRUSTY BREAD, TO SERVE (WE LIKE A
   FAT BAGUETTE)

YOU WILL ALSO NEED A BLENDER.

01 Slice the onion and fennel, keeping the fennel fronds (the green bits) in the fridge for later. Get your largest saucepan over a medium–high heat. Drizzle in a glug of olive oil. Add the veg along with a big pinch of salt. Fry, stirring occasionally, until softened and lightly browned.

02 Meanwhile, slice the garlic cloves. Add to the pan and fry for 30 seconds, then spoon in the fennel seeds and 1 teaspoon of smoked paprika. Squirt in the tomato purée and mix. Pour in the white wine and once it has bubbled away by half, tip in the plum tomatoes and fish stock. Half-refill the tin with water and pour in. Squash the tomatoes with your spoon. Bring the sauce to the boil then leave bubbling for 30 minutes.

03 Yoghurt time. In a small bowl stir the remaining paprika into the yoghurt, finely grate in the lemon zest, cut the lemon in half then squeeze in the juice of one half. Season with salt and black pepper to taste. Add a splash of water to make the yoghurt a drizzling consistency. Set aside.

04 Next, sort your mussels. Soak in a bowl of cold water, pull away any stringy bits ('the beards') and discard of any mussels that don't shut when pressed together in your hand. Cut the fish fillets into chunky pieces and season with salt.

05 Come back to your sauce. Blitz until velvety smooth using a blender and season with salt and black pepper to taste. Put the saucepan back over a medium high heat and bring to a rolling simmer.

06 Drop the mussels, fish and prawns into the pan. Cover with a lid and cook for 5–6 minutes until everything is completely cooked: the mussels will have opened, the prawns turned completely pink and the fish white and beginning to flake. Cut the remaining lemon half into wedges.

07 Divide the fish stew between four bowls. Spoon over the yoghurt, scatter over the basil leaves and the fennel fronds. Serve with the lemon wedges and some crusty bread. Class.

2

FRESH

New takes on some of your
favourites and some ideas you
won't have tried before.

SRIRACHA CRISPY TOFU

VG, GF, DF · ⏱ 30 MINS · SERVES 4

Coating your tofu in cornflour before you fry it is a great
kitchen hack to attain an optimal level of tofu crispiness. Pile up your
golden blocks like you're playing a delicious game of Jenga, and
pour over your sticky Sriracha and soy glaze. Ready in 30 minutes.
A firm favourite of our recipe testers.

GLUTEN-FREE: If you're cooking gluten-free, substitute the soy sauce for tamari.

BUDGET HACK: Omit the sesame seeds.

300G (10½OZ) BASMATI RICE

2 × 280G (10OZ) FIRM TOFU (WE LIKE THE TOFOO CO. NAKED TOFU)

200G (7OZ) TENDERSTEM BROCCOLI

1 LIME

2 SPRING ONIONS (OPTIONAL)

5 TBSP CORNFLOUR

3–4 TBSP SRIRACHA

1½ TBSP MAPLE SYRUP

6 TBSP SOY SAUCE

1 TBSP SESAME SEEDS

A HANDFUL OF FRESH CORIANDER

SALT AND BLACK PEPPER

VEGETABLE OR SESAME OIL

01   Cook the rice according to the packet instructions.

02   Meanwhile drain the tofu and cut into cubes. Cut each broccoli stem into three pieces and the lime into four wedges. Thinly slice the spring onions if using.

03   Spoon the cornflour into a bowl and season with salt and black pepper. Toss the tofu and the broccoli in the cornflour so that they get an even coating.

04   Get a large non-stick frying pan over a medium–high heat. Drizzle in a good glug of vegetable or sesame oil. In two batches fry the tofu and broccoli for 5 minutes, turning regularly, until crisp and golden brown.

05   Put the Sriracha, maple syrup and soy into a small saucepan with 3 tablespoons of water over a medium heat. Cook for 3–4 minutes until sticky and bubbling.

06   Divide the rice between four bowls. Top each one with the crispy tofu and broccoli then pour over the sticky Sriracha sauce. Scatter over the sesame seeds and spring onions, tear over the coriander and serve with the lime wedges.

MISO CABBAGE POKE BOWLS

VG, GF, DF · ⏱ 40 MINS · SERVES 4

The miso tahini dressing with grated fresh ginger and rice wine vinegar is an absolute revelation here – a lovely sophisticated sauce that shows off the range that cabbage can have. Served with lightly pickled cucumbers, fresh avo slices and fat edamame beans on a bed of seasoned sushi rice? Yep, this is a fresh one, folks.

GLUTEN-FREE: Check the labels of the white miso and tahini if cooking gluten-free and find an alternative if needed.

BUDGET HACK: Substitute the chilli oil for a big pinch of dried chilli flakes instead. Use basmati rice.

300G (10½OZ) SUSHI RICE

5 TBSP RICE WINE VINEGAR

2 TSP CASTER SUGAR, PLUS A PINCH

THUMB-SIZED PIECE OF FRESH GINGER

2 TBSP WHITE MISO

3 TBSP TAHINI

½ SMALL WHITE CABBAGE

1 LARGE CARROT

200G (7OZ) RADISHES

1 CUCUMBER

1 TSP CHILLI OIL WITH SEDIMENT (WE
    LIKE LEE KUM KEE), PLUS EXTRA TO
    SERVE

200G (7OZ) FROZEN EDAMAME BEANS

2 AVOCADOS

SALT AND BLACK PEPPER

01   Cook the sushi rice according to the packet instructions. Keep warm.

02   Mix 2 tablespoons of the rice wine vinegar with the caster sugar and a good pinch of salt in a small bowl. Set aside, this is your sushi seasoning.

03   Slaw time. Peel the ginger, then finely grate into a large bowl. Add the miso, tahini, 2 tablespoons of rice wine vinegar and 3 tablespoons of water. Stir everything together to create a creamy dressing then season with salt and black pepper to taste. Thinly shred or coarsely grate the white cabbage and carrots. Scrape into the bowl. Thinly slice the radishes and add them too. Toss everything to combine.

04   Using a peeler, peel the cucumber into long strips (save the core for sandwiches) into a separate bowl. Add the remaining tablespoon of rice wine vinegar, chilli oil and a big pinch of sugar and salt. Mix well.

05   Cook the edamame beans in a microwave or in a pan of boiling water then drain. Cut the avocados in half, remove the pits and cut into slices. Season with salt and black pepper.

06   Assembly time. Stir the sushi seasoning into the rice then divide between four bowls. Top each one with the slaw, cucumber, edamame and avocado, keeping each component in an individual pile to serve. Drizzle with extra chilli oil, if you like.

SPAGHETTI & MEATBALLS IN NDUJA SAUCE

⏱ 1 HR 15 MINS · SERVES 4

A MOB take on spaghetti and meatballs. Sausage meat makes the meatballs extra juicy. With the 'Nduja sauce, it's a straight 10/10.

BUDGET HACK: If you can't find nduja, fry off half a ring of chorizo, chopped up small, with the onion and add 1–2 teaspoons of chilli flakes into the sauce with the garlic instead.

6 PORK SAUSAGES

400G (14OZ) BEEF MINCE

2 ONIONS

3 FAT GARLIC CLOVES

150G (5½OZ) NDUJA

2 × 400G (14OZ) TINS OF CHOPPED
    TOMATOES

500G (1LB 2OZ) SPAGHETTI

A HANDFUL OF FRESH BASIL

OLIVE OIL

SALT AND BLACK PEPPER

PARMESAN CHEESE, TO SERVE

01   Squeeze the sausages from their skins into a large bowl. Add in the beef mince and finely grate in 1 onion. Season generously with salt and black pepper, mix together then use your hands to shape into 20 large meatballs. Place on a baking sheet.

02   Get a large non-stick frying pan over a medium–high heat. Drizzle in some olive oil and fry the meatballs for 5–6 minutes, in batches if you need to, until evenly browned. Set aside on a tray.

03   Reduce the heat to low. Finely chop the remaining onion, scrape into the pan, along with a drizzle more oil if needed. Turn up the heat to medium and fry, stirring occasionally, until soft. Finely chop the garlic.

04   Add the garlic and tear the nduja into the pan. Fry, smooshing with the back of your spoon to break it up until the nduja is pretty much melted. Tip in the chopped tomatoes along with half a tin of water. Bring the sauce to the boil, lower the heat and simmer away while you cook the spaghetti. Season with salt and black pepper.

05   Get a large saucepan of salted water on to boil, then drop in the spaghetti. Cook for 1 minute less than the packet instructions say to.

06   Add the meatballs back into the sauce. Simmer for 5 minutes, then flip each one over and continue to cook until the spaghetti is done.

07   When the pasta is cooked, drain in a sieve or colander but save a half of a mugful of the cooking water. Tip the pasta back into the saucepan. Push all the meatballs to one side and spoon the sauce into the spaghetti. Toss together, adding a little pasta water to create a silky sauce.

08   Divide the spaghetti and sauce between four bowls. Top each with five meatballs, tear over the basil and serve with a hunk of Parmesan on the side ready for grating over. Heaven.

ULTIMATE HUMMUS BOWL

V · ⏱ 50 MINS · SERVES 4

Nothing beats a bowl of creamy hummus. Need a quick snack? *How about hummus?* Need something faff-free for dinner? *Have you heard about hummus?* Warming the chickpeas and using a lot of tahini are our top tips for getting that silky texture. Serve with homemade za'atar flatbreads, pickles and harissa olive oil. Sorted.

MAKE IT VEGAN: By subbing out the flatbreads for pitta instead. Cut into triangles, toss with olive oil and za'atar in a large baking tray. Bake at 200°C/180°C fan/gas mark 6 for 10 minutes until crisp.

BUDGET HACK: Buy flatbreads.

300G (10½OZ) SELF-RAISING FLOUR
200G (7OZ) GREEK YOGHURT
2 TBSP ZA'ATAR, PLUS 1 TSP TO SERVE
1 TSP SALT
2 × 400G (14OZ) TINS OF CHICKPEAS
2 LEMONS
1½ TSP GROUND CUMIN
8 TBSP TAHINI
1 SMALL GARLIC CLOVE (OPTIONAL)
200G (7OZ) RADISHES
1–2 TBSP HARISSA
A HANDFUL OF PICKLED CHILLIES
SALT AND BLACK PEPPER

YOU WILL ALSO NEED A FOOD
PROCESSOR AND A ROLLING PIN.

01   Flatbread time. Measure the flour, Greek yoghurt, 2 tablespoons of za'atar and salt into a large bowl. Pour in 2 tablespoons of cold water and mix together to form a dough. If it looks dry, add an extra tablespoon of water. Tip the dough out onto a lightly-floured surface and knead for 2 minutes until smooth. Cover with a tea towel and leave to rest.

02   For the hummus, tip the chickpeas along with their water into a saucepan and gently heat (warmed chickpeas = creamiest hummus).

03   Ladle the chickpeas, along with a little of their water, into a food processor (if you have a small one you will have to do this in two batches). Cut the lemons in half. Add the cumin, tahini, garlic if using and squeeze in the juice of one lemon. Blitz for 2–3 minutes until completely smooth. Season to taste with salt and black pepper, adding a little more lemon if you like and chickpea water if you want a looser texture.

04   Thinly slice the radishes and scrape into a bowl. Squeeze over the remaining lemon juice and season with salt. Set aside to quick-pickle.

05   Cut your dough into eight pieces. Using a rolling pin, roll the dough out on a floured surface into oval flatbreads around 5mm (¼in) thick.

06   Get a large non-stick frying pan super-hot over a high heat. Cook the flatbreads one at a time, for 2 minutes on each side until they have bubbled up and are a little charred in places. Once cooked, pile the flatbreads on top of each other inside a tea towel and sprinkle with a little water – this will keep them squidgy.

07   Spoon the hummus into a large serving bowl. Drizzle over a good amount of olive oil and swirl the harissa on top. Pile a handful of pickled chillies to one side along with the quick-pickled radishes and sprinkle over the remaining za'atar. Serve with the flatbreads.

CHICKEN GYROS

⏱ 2 HRS + MARINATING OVERNIGHT · SERVES 4

You are going to love this one. Tenderized chicken is marinated in
spiced yoghurt overnight then roasted on an ingeniously constructed
homemade spit to bring a traditional taverna vibe into your own kitchen.
Of course, no gyros would be complete without some garlicky tzatziki,
oven chips, and fluffy pittas. If you want to go that extra mile, use
our recipe on page 58 to make your own pittas.

BUDGET HACK: Remove the smoked paprika and cumin and go for a more simple oregano yoghurt marinade instead.

3 GARLIC CLOVES

500G (1LB 2OZ) GREEK YOGHURT

1 TBSP DRIED OREGANO

1 TSP SMOKED PAPRIKA

1 TSP GROUND CUMIN

2 LEMONS

1KG (2LB 4OZ) BONELESS SKINLESS
    CHICKEN THIGHS

1 LARGE RED ONION

4 LARGE HANDFULS OF OVEN FRIES

1 LARGE CUCUMBER

A HANDFUL OF FRESH MINT

4 TOMATOES

8 PITTAS → HEAD TO PAGE 58 TO MAKE
    YOUR OWN

OLIVE OIL

SALT AND BLACK PEPPER

CHILLI SAUCE, TO SERVE (OPTIONAL)

YOU WILL ALSO NEED BAKING PAPER,
A ROLLING PIN, A METAL OR LARGE
WOODEN SKEWER AND FOIL.

01   The night before, finely grate two garlic cloves into a large bowl. Mix in 250g (9oz) of yoghurt, dried oregano, paprika, cumin, the zest and juice of one lemon and 3 tablespoons of olive oil. Season generously with salt and black pepper.

02   Put the chicken thighs in between two sheets of baking paper, bash to a 1cm (½in) thickness using a rolling pin (this will help tenderize the meat). Add the chicken to the yoghurt mixture and stir well to combine. Cover and leave to marinate in the fridge overnight.

03   The next day, preheat your oven to 200°C/180°C fan/gas mark 6. If using a wooden skewer soak in warm water for 30 minutes.

04   Get the chicken out of the fridge. Cut the onion in half horizontally (not through the base). Put one half aside then cut the top off the other, so that you are left with a flat onion round – this is to be your gyros base.

05   Put the skewer through the base of the onion with the point facing up. Place the onion on a baking tray, with the skewer facing up like a homemade vertical spit. Skewer on the chicken thighs, rotating the one on top by 90 degrees each time as you add another piece of chicken. Roast in the oven for 1 hour 30 minutes until cooked through. Check the chicken after 1 hour and if it's looking nicely browned, cover in a foil tent for the remaining 30 minutes of cooking time.

06   Cook the fries around the chicken gyros, according to the packet instructions.

07   Tzatziki time. Coarsely grate half the cucumber into a sieve then use your hands to squeeze out as much moisture as you can. Tip into a small bowl. Add the remaining 250g (9oz) of yoghurt, finely grate in the

remaining garlic clove and lemon zest. Roughly chop the mint leaves and add to the bowl. Drizzle in some olive oil. Season with salt, black pepper and lemon juice to taste.

08   Thinly slice the remaining red onion, cucumber and tomatoes.

09   Come back to the chicken. Using a sharp knife, carefully shave the meat off the skewer. Keep the chips warm in a low oven and heat the pitta bread.

10   Assembly time. Place the pitta breads onto four plates. Open up each one and spread with half of the tzatziki. Layer on the tomatoes, red onion and cucumbers on top then pile on the chicken and chips. To serve, drizzle over the remaining tzatziki and chilli sauce, if you like. Absolute winner.

MOB PITTAS

VG, DF · ⏱ 2 HRS 30 MINS · MAKES 8

Making your own pittas is simpler than you think. The dough uses
plain flour and yeast, which is what gives the bread its characteristic
lightness, but don't worry if their shape isn't perfect. The taste
makes up for it. Freeze any leftovers for another time.

300ML (10½FL OZ) WARM WATER

1 × 7G (⅛OZ) SACHET OF FAST-ACTION
   YEAST

500G (1LB 2OZ) PLAIN FLOUR

1 TSP SALT

2 TBSP EXTRA-VIRGIN OLIVE OIL

YOU WILL ALSO NEED A ROLLING PIN.

01   Measure the water into a jug then tip in the yeast and mix well. Leave for 5 minutes.

02   Tip the flour, salt and oil into a bowl and pour in the yeasty water. Mix together really well with your hands or a wooden spoon until no lumps of flour are left. Tip out onto a floured surface and give it a good old knead for 10 minutes until really smooth. It may start off a little sticky but will get smooth and less sticky as you knead. Stick in a bowl, cover with cling film with a small hole poked into it and leave for 1½ hours.

03   Lightly dust the work surface with flour then tip the dough out of its bowl. Cut the dough into eight equal pieces then roll into neat balls. Take a ball, dust with some flour then use a rolling pin to roll out to form an oval shape that is 15cm (6in) long. Cover with a tea towel and repeat with the remaining dough. Leave the pittas covered while the oven heats up.

04   Stick a thick baking sheet or, if you're fancy, a pizza stone into the oven and heat to 250°C/230°C fan/gas mark 9.

05   Lightly flour the baking sheet or stone. Place four of the pittas onto the hot baking sheet or stone and bake for 8 minutes until puffed up and just lightly browned. Wrap the cooked ones in a tea towel whilst you cook the others. The tea towel will keep them light and squidgy, enjoy.

01 Measure the water in a jug, then tip into a bowl with the yeast.

02 Add the flour, salt and oil.

05 Knead until really smooth, then place in a bowl to prove.

06 Remove your dough from the bowl and cut into eight pieces then roll into neat balls.

03 Mix together really well with a spoon or your hands until no lumps of flour are left.

04 Tip out onto a floured surface.

07 Take a ball, dust with flour then grab your rolling pin.

08 Roll out to form an oval shape that is 15cm (6in) long.

KALE & ROASTED BROCCOLI CAESAR SALAD

⊙ 45 MINS · SERVES 4

We all know the best thing about a Caesar salad is the dressing and we've perfected it for you right here. It's creamy, punchy and zingy – it's everything you'd ever want from a dressing. Toss that bright emulsion with charred roasted broc, chunky golden croutons, and lemony kale, and you've got a salad for the ages on your hands.

BUDGET HACK: Use whatever mustard you have at home, adjusting the quantity to taste.

200G (7OZ) KALE

2 LEMONS

6 MEDIUM EGGS

½ × 50G (1¾OZ) TIN OF ANCHOVY FILLETS IN OIL

1 GARLIC CLOVE

2 TSP DIJON MUSTARD

30G (1OZ) PARMESAN CHEESE, PLUS EXTRA TO SERVE

4 THICK SLICES OF CRUSTY WHITE BREAD

400G (14OZ) TENDERSTEM BROCCOLI

OLIVE OIL

SALT AND BLACK PEPPER

YOU WILL ALSO NEED A FOOD PROCESSOR.

01   Preheat your oven to 220°C/200°C fan/gas mark 7.

02   Tip the kale into a large bowl. Cut the lemons in half. Squeeze over the juice of one lemon, season well with salt and black pepper. Give the kale a good squeeze with your hands – this will help it soften in the lemon juice. Set aside.

03   Dressing time. Measure 100ml (3½oz) of olive oil into a jug. Separate two of the eggs and put the yolks into a food processor (freeze the whites for another time). Add the anchovies, garlic and mustard to the egg yolks. Finely grate in the Parmesan cheese and add 2 tablespoons of your measured oil. Blitz to a paste. Pour in 2 tablespoons more of oil, blitz again. Keep doing this until all of the oil is used up, you will be left with a thick and creamy dressing. Season with salt, black pepper and the juice of half a lemon to taste. If the dressing is a little thick for your liking, add 1–2 tablespoons of water and briefly blitz again to loosen.

04   Tear the bread into fat croutons. Spread out into a single layer on a baking tray, drizzle over a generous amount of oil and season with salt and black pepper. Lay the broccoli out onto a separate baking tray and do the same. Roast both in the oven for 10–12 minutes until the broccoli is tender and the croutons golden and crisp.

05   Meanwhile, boil the remaining 4 eggs for 6½ minutes. Drain, rinse under cold water until cool enough to handle and peel.

06   Divide the kale, croutons and broccoli between four plates. Halve the eggs and add to the salads. Drizzle over the dressing then, using a peeler, top each salad with shavings of Parmesan to serve.

BROCCOLI PAD THAI

V, GF, DF · ⏱ 25 MINS · SERVES 4

A veggie take on one of our all-time favourites. Get the broccoli nicely
charred in a super-hot pan before you add the chilli and garlic for
maximum flavour. Seek out tamarind paste if you can, it's what gives the
sauce its distinctive sweet yet tangy kick.

GLUTEN-FREE: Substitute the soy sauce for tamari if cooking gluten-free.

MAKE IT VEGAN: Use 1 × 280g (10oz) block of extra-firm tofu instead of the eggs. Cut into cubes and fry along with the broccoli.

BUDGET HACK: This one's good to go MOB. Any changes will affect the flavour.

1 LARGE BROCCOLI HEAD

1–2 RED CHILLIES (DEPENDING ON HOW
   SPICY YOU LIKE IT)

3 GARLIC CLOVES

4 SPRING ONIONS

300G (10½OZ) FLAT RICE NOODLES

2 TBSP TAMARIND PASTE

4 TBSP SOY SAUCE

2 TBSP SOFT BROWN SUGAR

4 LARGE EGGS

4 LARGE HANDFULS OF BEANSPROUTS

1 LIME

A LARGE HANDFUL OF ROASTED
   SALTED PEANUTS

NEUTRAL OIL, SUCH AS VEGETABLE,
   SUNFLOWER OR GROUNDNUT

01   Cut the broccoli into medium-sized florets then roughly chop up the stalk too as it's the best bit. Thinly slice the chilli, garlic and spring onions (green and white parts).

02   Soak the noodles in a large bowl of boiling water. Leave for around 10 minutes until softened.

03   Mix the tamarind paste, soy sauce and brown sugar together in a small bowl. Crack the eggs into a separate bowl and whisk well with a fork to combine.

04   Get a large frying pan over a high heat. Drizzle in a good glug of neutral oil and add the broccoli. Fry for 5 minutes until beginning to char in places. Turn the heat down a little, scrape in the chilli and garlic, and cook for a further minute more.

05   Push the broccoli mixture to one half of the frying pan, then pour in the beaten egg. Fry for 1–2 minutes, breaking the egg up occasionally with your spoon as it cooks, so you are left with nice big flakes of scrambled egg.

06   Drain the noodles in a sieve and tip them into the pan along with the spring onions and beansprouts. Give everything a good mix together and pour in the sauce. Fry for 2–3 minutes more until the noodles are cooked through.

07   Cut the lime into four wedges and roughly chop the peanuts. Divide the pad Thai between four bowls, top with the peanuts and serve with the lime wedges for squeezing over.

SPICY CHICKEN KATSU

🕐 **45 MINS · SERVES 4**

A MOB fave, this dish cannot be beaten. Carrot and ginger are vital elements in the sweet and spicy katsu sauce. Pour it all over your perfectly craggy, crunchy fried chicken for a guaranteed good time.

BUDGET HACK: Combine the dried spices and use 2 tablespoons of hot curry powder instead.

400G (14OZ) BASMATI RICE

2 ONIONS

3 CARROTS

4 GARLIC CLOVES

THUMB-SIZED PIECE OF FRESH GINGER, PEELED

4 TSP CURRY POWDER

2 TSP CHILLI POWDER

8 TBSP PLAIN FLOUR

600ML (21FL OZ) CHICKEN STOCK

2 TBSP SOY SAUCE

2 TBSP SWEET CHILLI SAUCE

3 MEDIUM EGGS

200G (7OZ) PANKO BREADCRUMBS

8 SKINLESS BONELESS CHICKEN THIGHS

VEGETABLE OIL

01   Cook the rice according to the packet instructions. Keep warm.

02   Katsu sauce time. Chop up your onions, carrots, garlic and ginger. You want to cut the onions and carrots into nice little cubes, about 1cm (½in).

03   Add a good glug of vegetable oil to a large frying pan over a medium–high heat. Fry the onions and carrots for around 8 minutes until soft and caramelized. At this point, add the garlic and the ginger. Fry for a further 3 minutes then mix in the curry powder and chilli powder. Gradually stir in 2 tablespoons of the flour, so you don't get any lumps, then pour in your chicken stock.

04   Mix in the soy sauce and allow the katsu sauce to bubble down and thicken. You want to simmer it for 10 minutes so the flavour from the onions and carrots infuses. If it gets too thick, just add a splash more water. Once the sauce is the perfect pouring consistency, remove it from the heat and pass it through a sieve. Set the sieved veg aside.

05   Place the remaining katsu sauce back on the heat. Add the sweet chilli sauce and mix everything together. Cover the sauce and set aside.

06   Chicken time. Get out three bowls. Add the remaining flour into one. Crack and whisk the eggs into another one, then tip the breadcrumbs into the third bowl. Dip each chicken thigh in the flour, then the whisked egg and finally roll in the breadcrumbs.

07   Get a large frying pan over a low–medium heat and drizzle in a generous amount of oil. Add the thighs to the pan and fry each for 5 minutes on each side. Remove from the heat once the chicken is cooked through and the breadcrumbs are golden brown.

08   Divide the rice between four bowls. Slice up the chicken and serve on the rice with the sauce poured over the top and the veg on the side.

PRAWNS PIL PIL WITH CIABATTA

GF, DF · ⏱ 20 MINS · SERVES 4

These king prawns are cooked in olive oil laced with paprika and shed-loads of garlic, and then served with crusty ciabatta for mopping up all the oily goodness. It's holiday food, One bite and you'll practically be able to feel the sun beating down you and hear the soft hiss of an Orangina being opened nearby.

GLUTEN-FREE: If serving with bread, choose a gluten-free alternative.

BUDGET HACK: Use frozen then defrosted raw king prawns.

2 LOAVES OF CIABATTA → HEAD TO
    PAGE 140 TO MAKE YOUR OWN,
6 CLOVES OF GARLIC
1 LARGE RED CHILLI
2 × 165G (5¾OZ) PACKETS OF RAW
    PEELED KING PRAWNS → OR IF YOU
    WANT TO PUSH THE BOAT OUT
    BUY RAW KING PRAWNS IN THEIR
    SHELLS AND PEEL INSTEAD
300ML (10½FL OZ) EXTRA-VIRGIN OLIVE
    OIL
½ TSP SMOKED PAPRIKA
A SMALL HANDFUL OF FRESH PARSLEY
SALT AND BLACK PEPPER

YOU WILL ALSO NEED KITCHEN PAPER.

01   Heat the ciabatta in a low oven at 120°C/100°C fan/gas mark ½.

02   Finely slice the garlic cloves and the red chilli. Dry the prawns on kitchen paper and season with salt and black pepper.

03   Get a small saucepan over a medium heat. Pour in the olive oil and heat until just shimmering. You want the oil to be hot but not nuclear otherwise the garlic and chilli will burn.

04   Add the garlic and chilli. Fry for 1 minute until sizzling, then add the prawns. Cook, stirring occasionally, for a further 2–3 minutes until all the prawns have turned pink. Take the pan off the heat and stir in the smoked paprika.

05   Tip the prawns along with their oil into a serving bowl. Roughly chop the parsley and scatter over the top. Serve with the ciabatta for dunking into the flavourful oil.

MISO ONION SOUP WITH SESAME GRUYÈRE TOASTS

⏱ 1 HR 30 MINS · SERVES 4

Miso adds a complexity to this soup as its bold, umami savouriness makes the perfect counterbalance to the sweet jammy onions. Be sure not to rush the caramelization process, though, as that's where all the flavour comes from. Low and very, very slow. Adding a splash of water to your onions at the beginning of their cooking time is a great trick to help them soften without burning.

MAKE IT VEGGIE: By using vegetable stock instead.

BUDGET HACK: Rather than a large glass of white wine, use 2 tablespoons instead.

6 LARGE ONIONS
100G (3½OZ) SOFTENED BUTTER
4 TBSP WHITE MISO
1 LARGE GLASS OF WHITE WINE
    (250ML/9FL OZ)
1.3 LITRES (46FL OZ) BEEF STOCK
8 THICK SLICES OF BREAD (WE LIKE
    SOURDOUGH OR BAGUETTE)
150G (5¼ OZ) GRUYÈRE CHEESE
2 TBSP SESAME SEEDS
OLIVE OIL
SALT AND BLACK PEPPER

01   Thinly slice the onions. Get your largest saucepan over a medium high heat. Drizzle in a good slosh of olive oil. Scrape in the onions along with a big pinch of salt. Pour in 500ml (17fl oz) water. Leave the onions to cook away for around 40 minutes, stirring regularly, until completely soft and the water has evaporated.

02   Add half the butter and 3 tablespoons of miso to the pan. Keep cooking the onions, stirring regularly, for around 20 minutes, until they are sticky and deeply caramelized.

03   Pour the white wine into the pan. Once bubbled away by half, pour in the stock. Give everything a good stir and bring the soup to a boil. Lower the heat and simmer away while you make the toasts. *You can make the soup in advance and reheat.*

04   Preheat your grill to high. Put the bread onto a large baking sheet and toast under the grill until lightly golden on both sides. Set aside.

05   Mix the remaining butter and miso together. Spoon over the toasts and spread with the back of the spoon. Grate over the Gruyère cheese. Return to the hot grill until the cheese is melted and beginning to golden, then scatter over the sesame seeds. Place back under the hot grill until bubbling and browned.

06   Season the soup with salt and black pepper. Ladle between four bowls and top each with two of the Gruyère sesame toasts.

STICKY SHORT RIBS WITH SMACKED CUCUMBERS & RICE

DF, GF · ⏱ 4 HRS 30 MINS · SERVES 4

Cooking short ribs takes a lot of time and effort but, when done right, they're worth the hassle. We slow-braise our ribs in a stock with aromatics and gochujang (a Korean chilli paste) until the meat is pulling away from the bone. The sauce is then reduced to a spicy, slightly sweet glaze and the ribs are grilled so you're left with a charred, maillard crust on top and melt-in-the mouth meat nestled underneath.

GLUTEN-FREE: If you're cooking gluten-free, substitute the soy sauce for tamari.

BUDGET HACK: This one is for going all out, MOB. Not budget, but oh so worth it.

1 RED ONION

THUMB-SIZED PIECE OF FRESH GINGER

6 GARLIC CLOVES

4 LARGE SHORT RIBS ON THE BONE →
   PICK UP SOME NICE FAT ONES

750ML (1¼ PINTS) BEEF STOCK

2–3 TBSP GOCHUJANG (DEPENDING
   ON HOW SPICY YOU LIKE IT)

2 TBSP SOY SAUCE

4 TBSP RICE WINE VINEGAR

1 TBSP, PLUS 1 TSP CASTER SUGAR

1 LARGE CUCUMBER

300G (10½OZ) BASMATI RICE

2 SPRING ONIONS

2 TBSP SESAME SEEDS

SALT AND BLACK PEPPER

YOU WILL ALSO NEED BAKING PAPER, FOIL AND A ROLLING PIN.

01   Preheat your oven to 160°C/140°C fan/gas mark 3.

02   Cut the red onion into wedges. Slice the ginger (no need to peel) and smash five of the garlic cloves with the back of your knife. Chuck everything into a roasting tin large enough to fit in the short ribs. Season the meat generously with salt and black pepper and nestle into the tin.

03   Into the stock, add the gochujang, soy sauce, 2 tablespoons of the rice wine vinegar and 1 tablespoon of the caster sugar. Stir well to combine and pour over the ribs. Cover the tray with a layer of baking paper and then foil. You want to make sure it's tightly sealed. Roast in the oven for 3–3½ hours until meltingly tender. The meat should have come away from the bone and be soft to the touch.

04   Once the short ribs are ready, carefully lift them out onto a baking tray. Strain the sauce into a small frying pan, discarding the bits. Skim off the fat and set the ribs aside.

05   Get the sauce over a high heat and reduce for 10 minutes until thick and glossy. Turn off the heat.

06   Smacked cucumber time. Using a rolling pin, satisfyingly hit the cucumber until it begins to break then cut into rough pieces. Scrape into a bowl. Finely grate in the remaining garlic clove. Add the remaining vinegar and caster sugar. Season well with salt and toss to combine.

07   Cook the rice according to the packet instructions.

CONTINUED →

08   Preheat your grill to high. Thinly slice the spring onions (green and white parts).

09   Slide the short ribs under the hot grill for 5 minutes until beginning to char in places. Meanwhile, gently reheat the sauce. Spoon the sauce over the ribs and sprinkle over the sesame seeds. Slide back under the hot grill for a further 3–4 minutes until bubbling and sticky.

10   Divide the rice between four bowls. Top each with a sticky short rib and a pile of smacked cucumbers. Scatter over the spring onions to serve.

SALMON TIKKA NAAN WRAPS

⏱ 30 MINS · SERVES 4

This one is all about the textures. We love the way that the crackle of the spicy grilled salmon skin contrasts against the freshness of the lime-forward slaw, cooling yoghurt and sticky mango chutney. All encased in a warmed naan bread. Perfect.

BUDGET HACK: Use frozen then defrosted salmon fillets.

8 TBSP NATURAL YOGHURT

2–3 TBSP TIKKA MASALA CURRY PASTE (DEPENDING ON HOW SPICY YOU LIKE IT)

4 SKIN-ON SALMON FILLETS

200G (7OZ) RADISHES

2 YELLOW PEPPERS

4 SPRING ONIONS

1 RED CHILLI

1 SMALL BUNCH OF FRESH CORIANDER

2 LIMES

4 NAAN BREADS → HEAD TO PAGE 117 TO MAKE YOUR OWN

SALT AND BLACK PEPPER

MANGO CHUTNEY, TO SERVE

YOU WILL ALSO NEED FOIL.

01   Mix 4 tablespoons of yoghurt with the curry paste in a small bowl. Lay the salmon fillets on a baking tray lined with foil, skin-side down. Season with salt and black pepper then spoon over the curried yoghurt, making sure to coat both the top and sides. Leave for 10 minutes to marinate.

02   Meanwhile thinly slice the radishes, peppers, spring onions and red chilli. Scrape into a bowl. Roughly chop the coriander, add this too. Finely grate in the zest of one lime, then cut in half and squeeze in the juice. Mix everything together and season to taste with salt and black pepper.

03   Preheat your grill to high.

04   Slide the salmon under the hot grill for 8–10 minutes until cooked through. Heat the naan breads in the oven underneath.

05   Cut the other lime into four wedges. Divide the naan between four plates, spread over the remaining yoghurt, top with the veg then flake over the salmon fillets. Spoon over a little mango chutney and serve with the remaining lime wedges.

SWEET & SOUR CAULIFLOWER

VG, GF, DF · ⏱ 40 MINS · SERVES 4

We've cracked the secret to the best sweet and sour sauce in this plant-based riff on a Cantonese classic. It's sticky, unctuous and everything you'd want from a takeaway. Minus the awkward calling-up-the-restaurant-and-asking-them-if-they-have-any-vegan-options part. Grating fresh ginger into the rice adds an extra fragrance to the whole thing.

GLUTEN-FREE: If you're cooking gluten-free, substitute the soy sauce for tamari.

BUDGET HACK: Use apple cider vinegar instead of rice wine vinegar.

2 MEDIUM CAULIFLOWERS
5 TBSP KETCHUP
3 TBSP SOY SAUCE
225ML (7¾FL OZ) PINEAPPLE JUICE
75G (2¾OZ) LIGHT BROWN SUGAR
100ML (3½FL OZ) RICE WINE VINEGAR
1½ TBSP CORNFLOUR
300G (10½OZ) BASMATI RICE
300G (10½OZ) FROZEN PEAS
THUMB-SIZED PIECE OF FRESH GINGER
2 SPRING ONIONS
NEUTRAL OIL, SUCH AS VEGETABLE,
    SUNFLOWER OR GROUNDNUT
SALT AND BLACK PEPPER

01 Preheat your oven to 220°C/200°C fan/gas mark 8.

02 Cut the cauliflowers into medium-sized florets. Roughly chop the stalks and the leaves (the best bit in our opinion) then divide between two baking trays. Season well with salt and black pepper then drizzle with a good glug of neutral oil. Spread out into a single layer so everything cooks evenly. Roast for 25–30 minutes until tender and a little charred.

03 Sauce time. Measure the ketchup, soy sauce, pineapple juice, sugar and rice wine vinegar into a small saucepan. Place over a low heat and cook until the sugar has dissolved, then bring to the boil. Measure the cornflour into a small bowl, add 1 tablespoon of water and mix to a milky smooth paste. Pour the paste into the boiling sauce, stir it in and cook for 3–4 minutes until the sauce has nicely thickened. Keep warm.

04 Cook the rice according to the packet instructions. Once cooked, put the frozen peas into a bowl and pour over boiling water, leave to defrost for 1–2 minutes until the peas turn bright green. Drain in a sieve then tip into the rice. Finely grate in the ginger and stir everything together. Keep warm.

05 Thinly slice the spring onions (green and white parts).

06 Divide the rice between four bowls and top with the cauliflower. Pour over the sweet and sour sauce and scatter over the spring onions to serve.

UDON NOODLES WITH HOT OIL

VG, DF · ⏱ 10 MINS · SERVES 4

We've taken the tried-and-tested technique of pouring sizzling-hot oil over hand-pulled noodles and applied it to straight-to-wok udon noodles in this quick and comforting recipe. A simple dressing of garlic, soy sauce, rice wine vinegar, and a boatload of chilli flakes combine with the udon and oil to make the most delicious sauce.

BUDGET HACK: This one is good as it is.

4 PAK CHOI

3 SPRING ONIONS

2 FAT GARLIC CLOVES

6 TBSP SOY SAUCE

4 TBSP RICE WINE VINEGAR

2–3 TBSP CHILLI FLAKES (DEPENDING ON HOW SPICY YOU LIKE IT)

8 TBSP NEUTRAL OIL, WE LIKE VEGETABLE, SUNFLOWER OR GROUNDNUT

2 × 300G (10½OZ) PACKETS OF STRAIGHT-TO-WOK UDON NOODLES

2 TBSP SESAME SEEDS

01 Bring a large saucepan of water to the boil. Cut the pak choi into quarters lengthways and thinly slice the spring onions.

02 Peel and finely grate the garlic into a small bowl, add the soy sauce, rice wine vinegar and chilli flakes. Add the neutral oil into a small saucepan.

03 Drop the pak choi into the pan of boiling water. Cook for 1 minute. Break the noodles up with your hands then drop into the water with the pak choi. Cook for 1 minute more and drain in a sieve.

04 Divide the noodles and pak choi between four bowls and top each one with spoonfuls of the garlic, chilli and soy sauce mix. Scatter over the spring onions and sesame seeds.

05 Get the saucepan of oil over a high heat. Once shimmering pour the oil equally into the four bowls to serve. Let people mix the oil into the noodz themselves.

HALLOUMI & GRILLED PEACH BURGERS

V · ⏱ 35 MINS · SERVES 4

This is our favourite veggie burger to date: jammy peaches,
salty halloumi, quick-pickled onions and smoky chipotle mayo all
get along famously in a soft and chewy brioche bun. Grilling
the peaches and halloumi on baking paper is the secret to
getting the best char with none of the stick.

VEGGIE: Check the label of the halloumi if cooking veggie and find an alternative if needed.

BUDGET HACK: Use chilli powder to taste, rather then chipotle, in the mayonnaise.

1 RED ONION

2 LIMES

4 TBSP MAYONNAISE

1–2 TBSP CHIPOTLE PASTE

2 RIPE PEACHES

1 AVOCADO

2 × 225G (8OZ) BLOCKS OF HALLOUMI

4 BRIOCHE BUNS

A HANDFUL OF BASIL

SALT AND BLACK PEPPER

OVEN CHIPS, TO SERVE

YOU WILL ALSO NEED BAKING PAPER.

01   Thinly slice the red onion and scrape into a small bowl. Cut one lime in half and squeeze the juice into the bowl. Season and scrunch with your hands as this will help the onion quick-pickle. Set aside.

02   Finely grate the zest of the remaining lime into a small bowl. Spoon in the mayo and as much chipotle paste as you like. Stir everything together and season with salt and black pepper.

03   Cut the peaches and avocado in half, remove the pits and cut the flesh into thick slices. Squeeze the remaining lime juice over the avocado. Cut both blocks of halloumi into thick slices.

04   Get a large griddle pan over a high heat. Tear a piece of baking paper the same size as the griddle pan and place it in the pan (the paper stops the peaches from sticking to the pan). Lay the peach slices on top and season with salt and black pepper. Griddle for 2 minutes on each side until nicely bar-marked and beginning to get jammy. Set the slices aside on a plate.

05   Tear a new sheet of baking paper to go onto the griddle pan and place the halloumi on top. Griddle for 2–3 minutes on each side. Meanwhile cut the brioche buns in half and lightly toast.

06   Assembly time. Spread the chipotle mayo on each bottom bun half. Top with the basil, avocado, griddled peach and halloumi. Finish with the quick-pickled onions and the brioche bun lids. Serve with oven chips.

COD & CHORIZO NEW POTATO TRAYBAKE WITH HOMEMADE AIOLI

GF, DF · ⏱ 1 HR 10 MINS · SERVES 4

It couldn't be easier to make your own uber-garlicky, lemony aioli by hand. It's the perfect condiment to stand up to the meaty fish and chorizo in this warming traybake.

GLUTEN-FREE: Check the label of the chorizo if you're cooking gluten-free and find an alternative if needed.

BUDGET HACK: Use a cheaper sustainable white fish such as pollock.

1KG (2LB 4OZ) NEW POTATOES

2 RED ONIONS

3 MIXED PEPPERS

225G (8OZ) CHORIZO RING

1 TBSP FENNEL SEEDS

2 TSP SMOKED PAPRIKA

1 BULB GARLIC

4 BONELESS SKINLESS COD FILLETS

2 LEMONS

2 EGG YOLKS → FREEZE THE WHITES TO BE USED ANOTHER TIME

150ML (5FL OZ) VEGETABLE OIL

1 SMALL GLASS OF SHERRY OR WHITE WINE (125ML/4FL OZ)

1 SMALL BUNCH OF FRESH PARSLEY

OLIVE OIL

SALT AND BLACK PEPPER

01   Preheat your oven to 200°C/180°C fan/gas mark 6.

02   Cut the new potatoes in half. Thickly slice the onions, peppers and chorizo. Add to your largest roasting tin (or two small tins). Drizzle with olive oil, add the fennel seeds, smoked paprika and season with salt and black pepper. Toss together. Nestle in the garlic bulb then spread everything out into a single layer so it roasts evenly. Roast in the oven for 35–40 minutes until the potatoes are golden and cooked through.

03   Meanwhile season the top of the cod with salt as this will keep the fish firm and succulent.

04   Mayonnaise time. Cut one of the lemons in half. In a medium-sized bowl squeeze in the juice of one lemon half and whisk with the egg yolks and a pinch of salt and black pepper. While whisking, pour in a tablespoon of vegetable oil. Once incorporated, add another tablespoon. Go really slowly, otherwise the oil and egg won't combine properly. You'll notice the yolks thickening and turning paler. Once this happens, you can pour in the oil more freely. Keep going until all the oil is incorporated. If it starts to look thick and greasy, add a splash of warm water to loosen.

05   Come back to your veg. Remove the garlic bulb. If spread across two tins, tip everything into one. Give everything a good toss and pour in the sherry or wine. Nestle the cod into the tin. Return to the oven for 12–15 minutes until the fish is cooked through.

06   Meanwhile squeeze the garlic out of its skin and add it into the mayo. Whisk, season with lemon juice, salt and black pepper to taste. Roughly chop the parsley and cut the remaining lemon into wedges.

07   Scatter the parsley over the tin, plonk in the lemon wedges and serve at the table with the homemade aioli.

CHICKEN CHOW MEIN

DF · ⏱ 25 MINS · SERVES 4

Thought that you could only get a good chow mein from your local
Chinese? Think again. This beauty is ridiculously simple to make and hits
all the right notes. A weeknight winner when you're pushed for time.

DAIRY-FREE: Check the stock
label if cooking dairy-free as
some stock contains traces
of milk.

BUDGET HACK: Replace the
Shaoxing wine and water with
150ml (5fl oz) of chicken stock.

4 TSP CORNFLOUR

**3 TBSP SOY SAUCE, PLUS A SPLASH TO
SERVE (OPTIONAL)**

3 TBSP OYSTER SAUCE

3 TBSP SHAOXING WINE

1 TSP SESAME OIL

1 TBSP CASTER SUGAR

4 SKINLESS CHICKEN BREASTS

400G (14OZ) EGG NOODLES

**½ CHINESE CABBAGE → IF YOU CAN'T
FIND, USE A SMALL WHITE CABBAGE
INSTEAD**

4 SPRING ONIONS

2 CARROTS

3 GARLIC CLOVES

4 LARGE HANDFULS OF BEANSPROUTS

VEGETABLE OIL

01   It's sauce time. Measure the cornflour into a bowl, add the soy
sauce and stir together until the cornflour is fully combined. Add the
oyster sauce, Shaoxing wine, sesame oil and sugar. Mix everything
together until you have a nice smooth sauce, then set aside.

02   Cut the chicken breasts up into bite-size pieces and tip into a bowl.
Spoon over 2 tablespoons of your sauce, toss and set aside to marinate.

03   Cook the egg noodles as per the packet instructions. Once ready,
drain in a sieve and leave in a bowl of cold water, ready for the wok.

04   Finely slice the cabbage, spring onions and carrots into matchsticks
then peel and slice the garlic finely.

05   Chow mein cooking time. This is a quick process so you want
everything prepared and ready by your wok. Get a wok or large frying
pan over a super-high heat. Drizzle in some vegetable oil. Chuck in
the chicken, fry for 2 minutes, stirring occasionally, then scrape in the
cabbage, spring onions carrots and garlic. Fry for 3 minutes more until
the veg is just soft and the chicken is cooked through.

06   Tip the noodles, beansprouts, remaining sauce and 100ml (3½fl oz)
of water into the pan. Give everything a good toss to coat in the sauce,
bubble away for 2 minutes then divide the chow mein between four
bowls. Serve with a splash more soy sauce if you like – quick comfort.

3

NOURISHING

Healthy-ish comfort dishes that will
leave you feeling good.

BUTTERNUT SQUASH PEARL BARLEY RISOTTO

V · ⏱ 1 HR 5 MINS · SERVES 4

We love the nutty, chewy texture of pearl barley with the sweetness of the caramelized squash here. Blitzing half the squash makes it super-creamy and as you add in all the stock at once it couldn't be easier

VEGGIE: Check the labels of the stock and Parmesan cheese if cooking veggie and find alternatives if needed.

BUDGET HACK: Use 2 tablespoons of white wine vinegar instead of the wine.

1 LARGE BUTTERNUT SQUASH

1 ONION

3 GARLIC CLOVES

300G (10½OZ) PEARL BARLEY

A SMALL HANDFUL OF FRESH THYME

1 LARGE GLASS OF WHITE WINE (250ML/9FL OZ)

1.6 LITRES (56FL OZ) VEGETABLE OR CHICKEN STOCK

3 TBSP PUMPKIN SEEDS

1 TSP SMOKED PAPRIKA

½ LEMON

A LARGE KNOB OF BUTTER

30G (1OZ) PARMESAN CHEESE, PLUS EXTRA TO SERVE

OLIVE OIL

SALT AND BLACK PEPPER

01   Preheat your oven to 200°C/180°C fan/gas mark 6.

02   Peel the butternut squash and cut into roughly 2cm (¾inch) cubes. Tip onto a large baking tray, drizzle with olive oil and season well with salt and black pepper. Toss together and spread everything out into a single layer so it roasts evenly. Place in the oven and roast for 35–40 minutes until soft. Set aside.

03   Meanwhile, peel and finely chop the onion and garlic. Get a large saucepan over a medium heat and drizzle in a good glug of olive oil. Scrape the onion in along with a pinch of salt and fry, stirring occasionally.

04   Add the garlic to the pan, cook for 1 minute more then tip in the pearl barley. Strip in most of the thyme leaves, discarding their sprigs. Give everything a good stir and pour in the white wine. Once bubbled away by half, pour in 1.4 litres (49fl oz) of stock. Bring to the boil, simmer on high for 30 minutes, stirring occasionally, until the liquid has been evaporated and the barley has a nice chewy bite. Reduce to a low heat.

05   Toast the pumpkin seeds in a dry frying pan over a medium heat. Once they begin to pop, drizzle in a little oil, add ½ teaspoon of the smoked paprika and season. Set aside.

06   Put half of the cooked squash into a food processor. Blitz with the remaining 200ml (7fl oz) of stock and smoked paprika until a smooth purée. Season with salt, black pepper and a little lemon juice to taste.

07   Stir the purée and cubes of butternut through the barley. Melt in the butter and grate in the Parmesan. Season with salt and black pepper.

08   Spoon the risotto into four bowls. Top with the pumpkin seeds, a good grating of Parmesan and a few thyme leaves to serve.

DAD'S PUTTANESCA

DF · ⏱ 30 MINS · SERVES 4

My dad used to cook this for me and my brothers all the time when
we were growing up, so I thought I'd share this website favourite with
you here. A perfect combination of store-cupboard ingredients and
lots of fresh parsley, this recipe is part of the reason that MOB Kitchen
exists today. Taste a bit of history. It's delicious. Ben x

BUDGET HACK: Use jarred olives
rather than fresh ones.

50G (1¾OZ) TIN OF ANCHOVY FILLETS
   IN OIL

1 BUNCH OF FRESH PARSLEY

2 TSP CHILLI FLAKES

2 FAT GARLIC CLOVES

2 TBSP CAPERS

A LARGE HANDFUL OF KALAMATA
   OLIVES

2 × 400G (14OZ) TINS OF PLUM
   TOMATOES

500G (1LB 2OZ) SPAGHETTI

OLIVE OIL

SALT AND BLACK PEPPER

01   Use a fork to get the anchovies out of the tin, roughly chop. Then
roughly chop the parsley (stalks and all).

02   Get a large frying pan over a medium–high heat. Add the anchovies
and chilli flakes to the pan with a tablespoon of olive oil and a tablespoon
of oil from the anchovy tin. Fry for 1 minute, stirring until the anchovies
have melted.

03   Peel then crush in the garlic cloves and add the chopped parsley
stalks. Mix everything together.

04   Add the capers and olives then tip in the plum tomatoes. Break
the tomatoes up with the back of a wooden spoon. Refill both the tins
halfway with water and add to the sauce.

05   Get your pasta on. Cook in a large pan of boiling salted water for 1
minute less than the packet instructions say.

06   Allow the sauce to reduce. Just when you are removing the pasta
from the heat, season the sauce with salt and black pepper and add a
large handful of chopped parsley.

07   Drain the pasta in a colander and tip into the saucepan with the
puttanesca sauce. Mix everything together and remove from the heat.
Divide the pasta into four bowls. Scatter over the remaining parsley
leaves and drizzle over some more olive oil to serve. Enjoy!

CURRIED FISH PIE

🕐 1 HR 20 MINS · SERVES 4

Fish and prawns covered in a fragrant and rich coconut sauce; mashed potato flecked with sweet slices of spring onions; and a cumin and mustard seed-spiced butter with some spinach and peas thrown in there for good measure. You're going to love this one.

MAKE IT GLUTEN-FREE: By using gluten-free flour.

BUDGET HACK: Leave out the king prawns. You could always add some more white fish instead.

1KG (2LB 4OZ) POTATOES

1 BUNCH OF SPRING ONIONS

THUMB-SIZED PIECE OF FRESH GINGER

2 GARLIC CLOVES

125G (4½OZ) BUTTER

3 TBSP CURRY POWDER

4 TBSP PLAIN FLOUR

2 × 400ML (14FL OZ) TINS OF COCONUT
    MILK

4 LARGE HANDFULS OF BABY SPINACH

1 TBSP CUMIN SEEDS

1 TBSP MUSTARD SEEDS

500G (1LB 2OZ) FISH PIE MIX

1 × 165G (5¾OZ) PACKET OF RAW
    PEELED KING PRAWNS

200G (7OZ) FROZEN PEAS

01   Preheat your oven to 220°C/200°C fan/gas mark 7.

02   Peel and quarter the potatoes. Tip into a large saucepan of cold salted water and bring to the boil. Once boiling, cook for 10-15 minutes until mashable.

03   Meanwhile, make the curried sauce. Thinly slice all the spring onions (green and white parts). Peel and finely grate the ginger and garlic. Place a medium saucepan over a medium heat, add 50g (1¾oz) of the butter in and let it melt. Once melted, add half the spring onions and all the ginger and garlic. Fry, stirring, for 1 minute. Spoon in the curry powder and flour, and fry for a further minute.

04   Gradually pour in the coconut milk, whisking as you go to keep the sauce lump-free. Bubble the sauce away for 5 minutes until nice and thick. Season to taste with salt and black pepper. Add the baby spinach, turn off the heat and set aside to wilt.

05   Come back to the potatoes. Drain them in a colander and steam-dry. Tip them back into their saucepan and mash. Melt the remaining butter in a small frying pan over a medium heat. Add the cumin and mustard seeds and fry for 30 seconds until the mustard seeds begin to pop. Pour the flavoured butter into the mash, add the remaining spring onions and mix well. Season with salt and black pepper.

06   Divide the fish pie mix, prawns and peas evenly over the bottom of a medium pie dish. Mix the spinach into the sauce then spoon over. Top with the spiced mash, using a fork to rough up the top and edges.

07   Bake in the oven for 25 minutes until piping hot. Preheat your grill to high. Slide the pie under the hot grill for 5 minutes until the mash is a little crisp and golden. Serve at the table and let people help themselves.

ONE-POT CHICKEN & BEAN CACCIATORE

GF, DF · ⏱ 1 HR · SERVES 4

We've taken the adage of 'more is more' to heart here and added white beans to an Italian classic to give you a proper one-pot full-course meal. The rosemary, olives and red wine are what gives the chicken its characteristic cacciatore flavour but we've also thrown in tinned cherry tomatoes for sweetness and a big splash of balsamic and chilli flakes for extra oomph. Who said you can't improve on perfection?

GLUTEN-FREE: If serving with bread, choose a gluten-free alternative.

BUDGET HACK: Use tinned olives, rather than fresh. Just make sure to give them a good rinse beforehand to remove some of the salt.

8 PIECES OF SKIN-ON, BONE-IN
   CHICKEN THIGHS AND DRUMSTICKS
2 RED ONIONS
4 GARLIC CLOVES
2 RED PEPPERS
½–1 TSP DRIED CHILLI FLAKES
4 FRESH ROSEMARY SPRIGS
2 TBSP TOMATO PURÉE
1 LARGE GLASS OF RED WINE
   (250ML/9OZ)
2 × 400G (14OZ) TINS OF CHERRY
   TOMATOES
2 × 400G (14OZ) TINS OF WHITE BEANS
   → WE LIKE CANNELLINI OR BUTTER
   BEANS
160G (5¾OZ) MIXED OLIVES
A SPLASH OF BALSAMIC VINEGAR
1 SMALL BUNCH OF FRESH PARSLEY
OLIVE OIL

SALT AND BLACK PEPPER

CIABATTA FOR MOPPING UP THE JUICES, TO SERVE (OPTIONAL) →
HEAD TO PAGE 140 TO MAKE YOUR OWN

01   Get your largest high-sided frying pan or casserole over a high heat. Drizzle in a good glug of olive oil. Season the chicken pieces generously with salt and black pepper then place skin-side down into the pan. Fry for 5–6 minutes, turning occasionally, until the skin is evenly golden. You may need to do this in two batches.

02   Meanwhile, peel the onions and garlic and thinly slice those and the peppers. Once the chicken is nicely browned, set aside on a plate. Reduce the heat to medium and scrape the onions and peppers into the pan. Add a pinch of salt then fry, stirring occasionally, for 10 minutes until soft.

03   Scrape in the garlic, cook for 1 minute more then add the chilli flakes and rosemary. Stir together then spoon in the tomato purée. Give everything a good mix then pour in the red wine. Leave to bubble away until reduced by half, then tip in the tins of cherry tomatoes. Bring the sauce to the boil.

04   Drain the beans and add to the pan along with the olives. Season well with salt and black pepper then nestle the chicken pieces in. Put on a lid and leave to simmer away for 20 minutes. Remove the lid and cook for a further 10 minutes until the chicken is cooked through and the sauce has reduced slightly. Season with salt, black pepper and a splash of balsamic vinegar.

05   Roughly chop the parsley and scatter over the top. Serve at the table with a crusty ciabatta for people to help themselves.

SPICED RATATOUILLE WITH HALLOUMI CROUTONS

V, GF · ⏱ 55 MINS · SERVES

We've taken all the elements you love about a ratatouille (i.e. melt-in-the-mouth veg in a rich tomato sauce) and given it a twist by adding loads of whole spices. The nigella seed halloumi croutons make this a belter of a dish.

VEGGIE: Check the label of the halloumi if cooking veggie and find an alternative if needed.

GLUTEN-FREE: If serving with naan or chapatis, choose a gluten-free alternative.

MAKE IT VEGAN: By swapping out the halloumi for tofu and cooking in the same way.

BUDGET HACK: Leave out the bread. It's a generous feed as it is.

2 AUBERGINES
2 COURGETTES
3 MIXED PEPPERS
6 SPRING ONIONS
3 FAT CLOVES OF GARLIC
1 TBSP CUMIN SEEDS
2 TSP CORIANDER SEEDS
1–2 TSP DRIED RED CHILLI FLAKES
1 TSP, PLUS 1 TBSP NIGELLA SEEDS
2 × 400G (14OZ) TINS OF CHOPPED
   TOMATOES
2 × 225G (8OZ) BLOCKS OF HALLOUMI
OLIVE OIL
SALT AND BLACK PEPPER
NAAN OR CHAPATIS, TO SERVE
   (OPTIONAL)

01   Cut the aubergines, courgettes and mixed peppers into medium-sized pieces. Season well with salt and black pepper.

02   Get your largest saucepan over a high heat and drizzle in a good glug of olive oil. Chuck in a third of your veg. Fry for 5 minutes, stirring occasionally, until beginning to soften. Transfer to a bowl and repeat. Tip all the veg out of the pan.

03   Finely slice four of the spring onions and peel and chop the garlic cloves. Put the saucepan back over the heat and drizzle in a little more oil. Scrape in the spring onions and garlic, cook for 1 minute then add the cumin and coriander seeds, chilli flakes and 1 teaspoon of the nigella seeds. Cook for 30 seconds until everything smells amazing then tip all your veg back into the pan.

04   Add the tins of tomatoes. Refill one tin with water and pour that in too then give everything a good stir. Bring to the boil, turn down the heat and leave the ratatouille to simmer away for 45–50 minutes until all the veg is completely cooked. Season to taste with salt and black pepper.

05   Halloumi time. Cut into cubes and chuck into a bowl. Add the remaining nigella seeds and toss to coat. Get a large non-stick frying pan over a high heat. Fry the halloumi for 2–3 minutes, turning regularly, until golden and crisp. Finely slice the remaining spring onions.

06   Divide the ratatouille between four bowls. Top with the halloumi croutons and scatter over the remaining spring onions. Serve with naan or chapatis, if you like.

COCONUT FISH CURRY

GF, DF · ⏱ 30 MINS · SERVES 4

This fragrant coconut curry is packed full of fragrant whole spices, caramelized red onion and sweet-as-can-be sugar snaps. Make sure to use a firm white fish like hake, as it will keep its meaty texture when cooked in the sauce.

BUDGET HACK: Use a curry powder (check the label if cooking gluten-free) instead of all the different spices. It won't have quite the same flavour but will be cheaper.

2 RED ONIONS

300G (10½OZ) BASMATI RICE

3 FAT GARLIC CLOVES

THUMB-SIZED PIECE OF FRESH GINGER

1 SMALL BUNCH OF FRESH CORIANDER

1 TBSP CUMIN SEEDS

1 TBSP MUSTARD SEEDS

2 TSP CORIANDER SEEDS

2 TSP CHILLI FLAKES

2 TSP GROUND TURMERIC

2 × 400ML (14FL OZ) TINS OF COCONUT
    MILK

4 BONELESS SKINLESS FIRM WHITE
    FISH FILLETS (WE LIKE HAKE)

200G (7OZ) SUGAR SNAP PEAS

1 RED OR GREEN CHILLI → SEEDS
    REMOVED IF YOU DON'T LIKE IT HOT

1 LIME

NEUTRAL OIL, SUCH AS VEGETABLE,
    SUNFLOWER OR GROUNDNUT

01   Peel and thinly slice one and a half onions. Get a large saucepan over a medium heat. Drizzle in a good glug of neutral oil and scrape in the onion along with a pinch of salt. Fry until soft, stirring occasionally, for around 8 minutes.

02   Meanwhile, cook the rice according to the packet instructions. Once cooked, keep warm.

03   Finely grate the garlic and ginger then finely chop the coriander stalks. Add to the onion pan, cook for 1 minute more then spoon in all the spices. Give everything a good mix, cook for 30 seconds or so until smelling unreal then pour in the coconut milk. Bring the curry to a boil.

04   Cut the fish fillets into large chunks, season well with salt and black pepper. Turn down the heat on the curry to a gentle simmer. Drop in the fish and sugar snap peas. Cook for 3–4 minutes until the fish is just cooked through and flaking into large chunks.

05   While the fish is cooking, finely chop the chilli and remaining red onion. Roughly chop the coriander leaves. Cut the lime into four wedges.

06   Season the curry with salt and black pepper. Divide the rice between four bowls. Ladle over the curry and top with the chilli, red onion and coriander leaves. Serve with the lime wedges for squeezing over.

SATAY-STUFFED SWEET POTATOES

VG, DF, GF · ⏱ 1 HR · SERVES 4

A loaded sweet potato is about as nourishing as it gets, MOB. The satay sauce in this banging dinner is spiked with chilli flakes and given a fair old whack of creamed coconut for extra creaminess. Garlic and ginger-fried greens round everything off nicely. A real favourite.

GLUTEN-FREE: If cooking gluten-free, substitute the soy sauce for tamari.

BUDGET HACK: Use frozen peas instead of the sugar snaps.

4 SWEET POTATOES

50G (1¾OZ) CREAMED COCONUT (¼ OF A BLOCK)

1 TSP CHILLI FLAKES, PLUS EXTRA TO SERVE

4 TBSP PEANUT BUTTER (SMOOTH OR CHUNKY IS FINE)

2 TBSP SOY SAUCE

200G (7OZ) TENDERSTEM BROCCOLI

THUMB-SIZED PIECE OF FRESH GINGER

2 FAT GARLIC CLOVES

200G (7OZ) KALE

200G (7OZ) SUGAR SNAP PEAS

1 LIME

OLIVE OIL

NEUTRAL OIL, SUCH AS VEGETABLE, SUNFLOWER OR GROUNDNUT

SALT AND BLACK PEPPER

01   Preheat your oven to 200°C/180°C fan/gas mark 4.

02   Prick the sweet potatoes all over with a knife and put onto a baking tray. Drizzle with olive oil and season generously with salt and black pepper. Roast in the oven for 45 minutes–1 hour, depending on size, until tender.

03   Meanwhile, make your satay sauce. Put the creamed coconut into a small saucepan. Add the chilli flakes, peanut butter and 1 tablespoon of soy sauce then pour in 250ml (9fl oz) of boiling water. Put the pan over a low heat and cook, stirring for 2–3 minutes until the coconut has melted and you are left with a rich satay sauce. Set aside to be reheated later.

04   When the sweet potatoes have 10 minutes to go, start on your greens. Cut the broccoli into three pieces and finely grate the ginger and garlic.

05   Get a large frying pan over a high heat. Drizzle in a good splash of neutral oil, then add the broccoli and fry for 4 minutes. Add the ginger and garlic to the pan. Cook, stirring for 30 seconds more, then tip in the kale and sugar snap peas. Pour in 100ml (3½fl oz) of water, cook for 3 minutes more, stirring occasionally until the kale has just wilted and the water is evaporated. Take off the heat.

06   Reheat the satay sauce. Finely grate in the lime zest, then cut the lime in half and squeeze in the juice of one half. Squeeze the remaining half into the greens and pour in the remaining soy sauce.

07   Get the potatoes out of the oven. Cut them in half and divide between four bowls. Spoon over half the satay sauce, then pile on the greens. Drizzle with the remaining satay sauce to serve and scatter with extra chilli flakes.

LAMB-STUFFED AUBERGINES IN HARISSA TOMATO SAUCE

GF · ⏱ 1 HR 15 MINS · SERVES 4

Cumin-spiced lamb mince is fried to crisp perfection, stuffed inside aubergines, and bathed in a sweet-yet-spicy cherry tomato, chickpea, and harissa sauce in this simple recipe. Heaven in a roasting tin.

NOTE: Grilling the aubergines before you roast them is the secret to making them meltingly tender.

BUDGET HACK: Swap the tins of cherry tomatoes for chopped tomatoes. Substitute pine nuts for pumpkin seeds.

4 AUBERGINES

1 ONION

2 FAT GARLIC CLOVES

400G (14OZ) LAMB MINCE

1½ TBSP CUMIN SEEDS

1 TBSP GROUND CORIANDER

2 × 400G (14OZ) TINS OF CHERRY
  TOMATOES

2 × 400G (14OZ) TINS OF CHICKPEAS

2 TBSP HARISSA, PLUS EXTRA TO SERVE

1 SMALL BUNCH OF FRESH PARSLEY

150G (5½OZ) NATURAL YOGHURT

50G (1¾OZ) TOASTED PINE NUTS

OLIVE OIL

SALT AND BLACK PEPPER

YOU WILL ALSO NEED FOIL.

01   Preheat your grill to high.

02   Cutting from the base, slice the aubergines in half lengthways, stopping two-thirds of the way up so that the stalk stays attached – this will create the pocket for your lamb stuffing.

03   Lay the aubergines into your largest roasting tin. Drizzle with olive oil and season with salt and black pepper. Slide under the hot grill for 15 minutes, turning halfway, until they start to collapse and soften. Set aside.

04   Meanwhile, peel and finely chop the onion. Get a frying pan over a medium heat. Drizzle in a good splash of olive oil, scrape in the onion along with a pinch of salt. Fry, stirring occasionally, until soft.

05   Peel and finely chop the garlic cloves. Add to the pan. Cook for 30 seconds more then dump in the lamb mince. Break up the mince with the back of your spoon. Turn up the heat to high and fry the lamb for around 8 minutes until browned and crisp. Sprinkle over the cumin seeds and ground coriander. Give everything a good stir and cook for a further minute. Then take off the heat and season with salt and black pepper.

06   Turn your oven to 200°C/180°C fan/gas mark 6.

07   Stuff the aubergines in the roasting tin with the spicy lamb mix. Tip the tins of cherry tomatoes in around the aubergines. Half fill one tin with water, spoon in the harissa and pour it into the roasting tin. Drain the chickpeas and add them too. Season with salt and black pepper, cover with foil, roast for 40 minutes until the aubergine is soft.

08   Roughly chop the parsley. Dollop spoonfuls of yoghurt on top of the aubergines and swirl through some harissa. Scatter over the pine nuts and parsley. Serve out of the tin for people to help themselves.

KALE & PEA ALOO WITH FRIED PANEER

V, GF · ⏱ 1 HR · SERVES 4

This is our take on a saag aloo, using a bag of kale and frozen peas instead of spinach. Fried curry powder-coated paneer and a zesty coriander and coconut chutney take things up a notch, transforming this simple dish into one that your MOB will want you to make time and time again.

GLUTEN-FREE: Check the label of your curry powder and if serving with naan choose a gluten-free alternative.

MAKE IT VEGAN: Swap the paneer for tofu and use coconut yoghurt instead of dairy.

BUDGET HACK: Don't use paneer.

1KG (2LB 4OZ) NEW POTATOES

1 SMALL BUNCH OF FRESH CORIANDER

4 TBSP DESICCATED COCONUT

150G (5½OZ) NATURAL YOGHURT

2 LIMES

1 ONION

3 GARLIC CLOVES

THUMB-SIZED PIECE OF FRESH GINGER

1 RED CHILLI

1 TBSP CUMIN SEEDS

3 TBSP CURRY POWDER

300G (10½ OZ) FROZEN PEAS

200G (7OZ) KALE

2 × 225G (8OZ) BLOCKS PANEER

NEUTRAL OIL, SUCH AS SUNFLOWER, VEGETABLE OR GROUNDNUT

SALT AND BLACK PEPPER

MANGO CHUTNEY, TO SERVE (OPTIONAL)

RICE OR NAAN, TO SERVE (OPTIONAL)

→ HEAD TO PAGE 117 FOR OUR HOMEMADE MOB NAAN RECIPE

01   Cut the new potatoes in half, or quarters if they are a bit big. Tip into a large saucepan of cold salted water and bring to the boil. Once boiling, cook for 8–10 minutes until tender (a knife should slide into them easily). Drain in a colander.

02   Meanwhile, make the raita. Blitz the coriander in a food processor (stalks and all) along with the coconut, yoghurt and zest and juice of one lime until you have a textured green dip. Season to taste. Set aside in the fridge.

03   Peel and finely chop the onion. Get your largest saucepan over a medium heat and drizzle in a good glug of neutral oil. Scrape in the onion along with a pinch of salt and fry, stirring occasionally, until soft. Meanwhile, peel and finely chop the garlic and ginger and finely chop the chilli. Add to the pan and fry for 1 minute more. Spoon in the cumin seeds and 2 tablespoons of the curry powder. Cook, stirring everything together, for a further 30 seconds then tip in the drained new potatoes.

04   Give everything a good mix to coat the potatoes in the spices, add in the peas and kale. Pour in 200ml (7fl oz) of water, leave to simmer away, stirring occasionally to allow the kale to wilt.

05   Cut the paneer into roughly 1cm (½inch) cubes. Tip into a small bowl, coat with 2 tablespoons of oil and the remaining curry powder.

06   Get a large non-stick frying pan over a high heat. Add the spiced paneer along with the oil. Fry for 3–4 minutes, turning regularly, until crisp and golden.

07   Cut the remaining lime into four wedges. Season the kale and pea aloo with salt and black pepper. Pile into four bowls, top with the fried paneer, a dollop of raita and some mango chutney, if you like. We like to eat this with a naan or rice.

CHICKEN LEMON & ORZO SOUP

DF · ⏱ 45 MINS · SERVES 4

Is there anything better than a bowl of chicken soup? How about a
bowl of chicken soup that's packed to the brim with al dente
oblongs of orzo and handfuls of garden-fresh herbs? The subtle aniseed
flavour from the tarragon is spot on with juicy chicken thighs.

DAIRY-FREE: Check the ingredients in your stock as some contain traces of dairy.

BUDGET HACK: Replace the tarragon and bay with 1 tablespoon of mixed dried herbs.

1 LARGE LEEK
2 CARROTS
2 CELERY STICKS
3 FAT GARLIC CLOVES
8 BONELESS SKINLESS CHICKEN
    THIGHS
2 TSP FENNEL SEEDS
4 BAY LEAVES
1½ LITRES (2½ PINTS) CHICKEN STOCK
100G (3½OZ) DRIED ORZO PASTA
A HANDFUL OF FRESH TARRAGON
1 LEMON
OLIVE OIL
SALT AND BLACK PEPPER

01   Thinly slice the leek, carrots and celery.

02   Get a large saucepan over a medium heat. Drizzle in a good glug of olive oil, scrape in the veg along with a big pinch of salt. Fry for 10 minutes, stirring occasionally, until softened.

03   Meanwhile, peel and finely chop the garlic cloves. Season the chicken thighs with salt and lots of black pepper.

04   Add the garlic and fennel seeds to the pan and fry for 30 seconds more. Chuck in the bay leaves and pour in the chicken stock. Bring to a boil, then reduce the heat and drop in the chicken thighs. Simmer for 15–20 minutes until the chicken is cooked through. When ready, transfer the chicken to a plate using tongs.

05   Bring the soup back to a boil, tip in the orzo pasta, cook for 8–10 minutes until it has just a little bite.

06   Shred the chicken thighs with two forks. Return the chicken to the soup to warm through. Remove the bay leaves and season with salt and black pepper. Roughly chop the tarragon.

07   Ladle the soup into four bowls. Scatter over the chopped tarragon and finely grate some lemon zest over each bowl. Cut the lemon into wedges and serve with the soup for squeezing over.

YELLOW DAL

VG, GF, DF · ⏱ 1 HR · SERVES 4

Nothing says comfort like a bowl of creamy, fragrant dal. And nothing
says it in a soft, dulcet tone quite like this dal right here. Simmering
the lentils in fresh ginger and turmeric gives those lovely little legumes
time to develop a more rounded flavour before you add the crispy
shallot, garlic, chilli-spiced tarka towards the end.

GLUTEN-FREE: If serving with naan, paratha or roti, choose a gluten-free alternative.

BUDGET HACK: Skip out on the fresh coriander.

LARGE THUMB-SIZED PIECE OF FRESH
    GINGER
400G (14 OZ) SPLIT MUNG DAL (YELLOW
    SPLIT LENTILS)
2 TSP GROUND TURMERIC
2 BANANA SHALLOTS
3 FAT GARLIC CLOVES
1 GREEN CHILLI
1 TBSP CUMIN SEEDS
1 TBSP MUSTARD SEEDS
A HANDFUL OF FRESH CORIANDER
1 LIME
NEUTRAL OIL, SUCH AS VEGETABLE,
    SUNFLOWER OR GROUNDNUT
SALT AND BLACK PEPPER
NAAN, PARATHA OR ROTI, TO SERVE
    → HEAD TO PAGE 117 FOR OUR
    HOMEMADE MOB NAAN RECIPE

01   Peel the ginger and cut into matchsticks.

02   Rinse the lentils in a bowl of cold water, use your fingers to massage the lentils. Once the water is cloudy, drain and repeat until the water is pretty much clear. Drain the washed lentils in a sieve and tip into a large saucepan. Pour in 2 litres (3½ pints) of cold water. Stir in the ginger, turmeric and a generous pinch of salt.

03   Get your saucepan over a high heat and bring the lentils to the boil. Once boiling reduce the heat to medium, simmer away for 30 minutes, stirring occasionally so it doesn't catch, until the lentils have broken down, most of the water has been absorbed and you are left with a creamy loose dal. Once you are happy with the consistency, season with salt and black pepper then reduce the heat to low to keep the dal warm.

04   Tarka time. Peel and finely slice the shallots and garlic, then finely slice the chilli. Get a small frying pan over a high heat. Drizzle in enough neutral oil that it just covers the surface of the pan. Scrape in the shallots and fry for 4–5 minutes, stirring regularly, until lightly golden. Add the garlic, chilli, cumin and mustard seeds. Cook for about 1 minute more, stirring continuously, until the shallots are just crisp and everything smells unreal. Take off the heat.

05   Divide the dal between four bowls and spoon over the hot tarka. Tear over some coriander leaves and cut the lime into wedges to serve. We like to eat this with a naan, paratha or roti.

MOB NAAN

V · ⏱ 1 HR 45 MINS · MAKES 4

A shop-bought naan doesn't even come close to the real thing. This lightly charred, pillowy-soft, onion seed bread is a revelation. Especially when brushed with melted ghee or butter. If you've never made bread before these are a brilliant starting point.

125ML (4FL OZ) WARM WATER

1 × 7G (⅛OZ) SACHET OF FAST-ACTION YEAST

300G (10½OZ) PLAIN FLOUR

1 TSP CASTER SUGAR

½ TSP FINE SEA SALT

2 TBSP NIGELLA SEEDS

125G (4½OZ) NATURAL YOGHURT

3 TBSP MELTED BUTTER OR GHEE

YOU WILL ALSO NEED A ROLLING PIN AND KITCHEN PAPER.

01   Measure the water into a jug on a set of scales then tip in the yeast and mix well. Leave for 5 minutes.

02   Tip the flour into a large bowl with the sugar, salt and nigella seeds and mix together. Make a well in the centre and pour in the yoghurt and the yeasty water. Mix well with your hands or a wooden spoon until a dough forms then transfer the mixture onto a well-floured work surface and knead, with floured hands, for 5 minutes or until smooth. Add back to the bowl, cover with cling film with a small hole poked into it and leave for around 1 hour until doubled in size.

03   Tip the dough back out onto a well-floured surface. Divide into four pieces and roll each into a ball. Flour each one and use a rolling pin to roll each of them out to form a teardrop shape that is 20cm (8in) long.

04   Heat a large frying pan over a really high heat until smoking and turn your oven on to low, 120°C/100°C fan/gas mark ½.

05   Place two naans at a time in the pan, topping and tailing them like the two sides of ying and yang. Fry for 2 minutes until puffed up and beginning to char, then flip and repeat. If the naans are looking a little dark, lower the heat slightly.

06   Chuck onto a baking tray and brush liberally with melted butter or ghee. Put into the oven to keep warm. Use a little kitchen paper to carefully wipe the pan clean then repeat with the remaining dough.

01 Tip the flour, sugar, salt and nigella seeds into a bowl and mix together.

02 Make a well in the centre and pour in the yoghurt and the yeasty water.

05 Knead, with floured hands, for 5 minutes or until smooth.

06 Divide into four pieces and roll each into a ball. Flour each one and use a rolling pin to roll each of them out.

03 Mix well with your hands or a wooden spoon until a dough forms.

04 Tip the dough out onto a well-floured work surface.

07 Form each into a teardrop shape.

08 Fry two at a time in the frying pan.

SMOKEY AUBERGINE & RED PEPPER CHILLI

VG, DF · ⏱ 1 HR · SERVES 4

One of our recipe testers said this is the best veggie chilli she'd ever tried. Which, considering the ridiculous amount of chilli she's consumed in her lifetime, is really saying something. Grilling the vegetables – plus the addition of some dark chocolate and a healthy spoonful of chipotle paste – is the secret to adding that extra oomph of flavour.

BUDGET HACK: Skip out the dark chocolate and use ½ teaspoon of instant coffee, mixed into a paste with 1 tablespoon of water instead.

2 AUBERGINES

3 MIXED PEPPERS

2 RED ONIONS

5 GARLIC CLOVES

2 TSP GROUND CUMIN

2 TSP DRIED OREGANO

2 TBSP CHIPOTLE PASTE, PLUS EXTRA
    TO SERVE (OPTIONAL)

2 × 400G (14OZ) TINS OF CHOPPED
    TOMATOES

2 × 400G (14OZ) TINS OF KIDNEY BEANS

2 SQUARES OF DARK CHOCOLATE

2 LIMES

1 SMALL BUNCH OF FRESH CORIANDER

1 BAGUETTE

4 BIG SPOONFULS OF YOGHURT →
    USE DAIRY-FREE IF WANT TO KEEP
    VEGAN

OLIVE OIL

SALT AND BLACK PEPPER

01   Preheat your grill to high.

02   Slice the aubergines, peppers and 1½ red onions into medium-sized chunks. Spread out onto your largest baking tray. Drizzle liberally with olive oil and add some salt and black pepper to season. Cook under the hot grill for 15 minutes, tossing the veg every 5 minutes, until collapsed and blackened in places.

03   Meanwhile, finely chop all the garlic cloves. Scrape two-thirds into a small bowl to be used later. Get a large saucepan over a medium heat and drizzle in a little oil. Add the remaining garlic, fry for 30 seconds and then spoon in the cumin and oregano. Cook for 30 seconds more. Add the chipotle paste and tip in the chopped tomatoes.

04   Drain the kidney beans and add to the pan. Refill one of the cans halfway with water. Pour that in too. Bring to the boil and season with salt and black pepper. Add the grilled veg and the chocolate to the pan. Give everything a good mix then leave the chilli to simmer away for 20 minutes.

05   Turn the oven to 200°C/180°C fan/gas mark 6.

06   Thinly slice the remaining onion half and scrape into a small bowl. Cut one lime in half and squeeze in the juice. Season and scrunch with your hands as this will help the onion quick-pickle. Set aside.

07   Finely chop most of the coriander and add to the bowl of chopped garlic. Pour in 4 tablespoons of olive oil. Slice the baguette on a diagonal, lay the bread onto a baking tray and spoon over the garlic oil. Bake in the oven for 10 minutes until crisp and golden.

08 Cut the remaining lime into four wedges. Season the chilli to taste and pile into four bowls. Top with a spoonful of yoghurt then scatter over the quick-pickled onions and remaining coriander leaves. Add a swirl more chipotle paste if you like things spicy. Serve with the garlic toasts and lime wedges. Banger.

CREAMED CORN CHOWDER, CHORIZO & PICKLED JALAPEÑOS

GF · ⏱ 55 MINS · SERVES 4

Fresh corn, potatoes, chicken stock, and double cream might
make this chowder a comforting hug in a bowl but it's the hot and
heavy sprinkling of spicy fried chorizo and jalapeños that add
a much-needed heat and fiery frisson to proceedings.

GLUTEN-FREE: Check the label of the chorizo if you're cooking gluten-free and find an alternative if needed.

BUDGET HACK: Use 2 × 340g (12oz) tins of sweetcorn instead.

1 ONION

2 CELERY STICKS

A KNOB OF BUTTER

3 FAT GARLIC CLOVES

2 LARGE POTATOES (APPROX. 500G/1LB 2OZ)

½ TSP CAYENNE PEPPER

1½ LITRES (2½ PINTS) CHICKEN STOCK

6 CORN ON THE COBS

150ML (5FL OZ) DOUBLE CREAM

225G (8OZ) CHORIZO RING

OLIVE OIL

SALT AND BLACK PEPPER

PICKLED JALAPEÑOS, TO SERVE

YOU WILL ALSO NEED A BLENDER.

01   Peel and finely chop the onion and celery. Get a large saucepan over a medium heat. Add the butter with a splash of olive oil and let it melt, then scrape in the veg. Add a pinch of salt. Fry, stirring occasionally, until soft.

02   Meanwhile, peel and finely chop the garlic cloves. Peel the potatoes and cut into smallish cubes. Add the garlic to the pan, fry for 30 seconds, then spoon in the cayenne pepper. Give everything a good stir and tip in the potatoes. Pour in the stock and bring to a slow boil.

03   Place a corn cob upright on your chopping board. Holding it in one hand, use your knife to cut down each side of the corn – the kernels should come off easily. Repeat until you've removed the kernels from all of the corn cobs. Add the corn to the soup. Simmer away for 15–20 minutes until the potatoes and corn are cooked through.

04   Ladle half of the soup into a bowl and blitz until smooth with a blender then pour it back into the pan – this will make your chowder extra creamy. Lower the heat to a gentle simmer. Stir in the cream and season with salt and black pepper to taste. Keep warm.

05   Chorizo time. Peel and chop the chorizo into rough cubes. Get a large frying pan over a high heat. Drizzle in a splash of olive oil, chuck in the chorizo and fry until crisp. Turn off the heat and set aside.

06   Roughly chop some pickled jalapeños. Ladle the soup into four bowls. Top each one with the pickled jalapeños and crispy chorizo, drizzling over its oil to finish.

4

INDULGENT

For those times you really want to get
stuck in. Some cheesy bangers here.

VODKA RIGATONI

V · ⏱ 30 MINS · SERVES 4

This is the only vodka pasta recipe you need in your life and one of the most popular recipes on our website for good reason. The key ingredients are simple: tomato purée, basil, and pasta water. A *lot* of pasta water. There's no other way.

VEGGIE: Check the label of the Parmesan cheese if cooking veggie and find an alternative if needed.

BUDGET HACK: This one is pretty cheap as it is, MOB.

1 ONION
3 GARLIC CLOVES
2 RED CHILLIES
150G (5½OZ) PARMESAN CHEESE (WITH RIND), PLUS EXTRA FOR GRATING
150G (5½OZ) TOMATO PURÉE
50ML (1¾FL OZ) VODKA
200ML (7FL OZ) DOUBLE CREAM
500G (1LB 2OZ) RIGATONI
1 BUNCH OF FRESH BASIL
OLIVE OIL
SALT AND BLACK PEPPER

01   Peel the onion and garlic. Finely slice the onion and red chillies. Grate the garlic. Chop off the Parmesan rind.

02   Drizzle in a splash of olive oil to a large saucepan followed by the onions. Fry until translucent then add the garlic and chilli. Fry for a minute, and then add the tomato purée. Mix it in and cook for 4 minutes over a medium heat, allowing the tomato mix to catch on the pan.

03   At this point, pour in the vodka, deglazing the sticky bits off the bottom of the pan with your wooden spoon. Once the alcohol has burned off (20 seconds), add the cream as well as the cheese rind. Mix it in and turn down the heat.

04   Get your pasta on. Cook in a large pan of boiling salted water for 1 minute less than the packet instructions say. After 2 minutes, remove 200ml (7fl oz) of pasta water from the pan.

05   Stir in 100ml (3½fl oz) of the pasta water into your vodka sauce (reserve the rest). Then grate in the cheese and add salt and black pepper. Mix it together and bubble on a low–medium heat for a few minutes until the cheese has melted.

06   Drain the pasta in a colander, then tip into the vodka sauce, tossing it through and adding splashes of reserved pasta water to keep the sauce loose.

07   Pile the pasta into four bowls. Tear over the basil and finish with some more grated cheese. Enjoy.

THE ULTIMATE CHEESEBURGER

🕐 1 HR · SERVES 4 · BY THOMAS STRAKER

The daddy of all burgers. Beef patty, crispy shallots, caramelized
onions and an incredible homemade burger sauce. Freshly ground meat
from a butcher is always best to use if you can. Pick the fattiest cut —
the higher the fat content, the juicier the burgers.

2 MEDIUM ONIONS

800G (1LB 12OZ) BEEF MINCE

4 BRIOCHE BUNS

8 SLICES OF RED LEICESTER OR
  CHEDDAR CHEESE

1 LARGE JAR OF PICKLES

VEGETABLE OIL

SALT AND BLACK PEPPER

FOR THE CRISPY SHALLOTS

2 SHALLOTS

1 TBSP CORNFLOUR

500ML (17FL OZ) VEGETABLE OIL

FOR THE BURGER SAUCE

1 SHALLOT

3 TBSP SWEET PICKLE RELISH

4 TBSP MAYONNAISE

2 TBSP KETCHUP

2 TBSP MUSTARD (I USE FRENCH'S)

A PINCH OF CAYENNE PEPPER

YOU WILL ALSO NEED KITCHEN PAPER.

01 Start with the caramelized onions. Peel and finely slice the onions. Place a medium saucepan over a medium heat and drizzle in a glug of olive oil. Add the onions and cook slowly for 5 minutes until soft. Add a good pinch of salt and then cook until caramelized for a further 5–10 minutes. Remove from the pan then set aside.

02 Next up, crispy shallots. Peel and finely slice your shallots. Add the cornflour into a bowl and toss the shallots through. Heat your vegetable oil in a pan to around 150°C/300°F and fry the shallots until golden brown. Drain on kitchen paper and season with salt. Set aside.

03 Time for the burger sauce. Peel and dice the shallots and mix with all the other ingredients in a bowl. Set aside in the fridge.

04 For the beef patty, season the meat with salt and black pepper and shape into four equal-sized patties.

05 Heat a heavy-based frying pan over a medium–high heat. Halve the buns and toast in the pan on each side until dark golden. Then set aside.

06 In the same hot pan, drizzle in a glug of vegetable oil. Season the burger patties with salt and put in the hot pan for around 2 minutes. While cooking, press the patty down firmly to get good crispy edges (if you are using a small pan do not overcrowd it, as you want to get good caramelization on the patty).

07 Flip the patty, add two slices of cheese to the top and put a lid on the pan to let the cheese melt.

08 Time to layer up. Slice your pickles and spread burger sauce on the bottom of the bun. Add the sliced pickles, then caramelized onions, the burger patty, followed by more burger sauce and finally the crispy shallots. Add your brioche lid on top and tuck in!

MOB'S CHEESY CHIPS

V, GF · ⏱ 1 HR 20 MINS · SERVES 4

Soph pretty much subsisted on a diet of cheesy chips while she was at school. We're bringing back the nostalgia with our very own chip shop-style gravy and curry sauce. Some dishes speak for themselves.

VEGGIE: Check the label of the mozzarella cheese if cooking veggie and find an alternative if needed.

GLUTEN-FREE: Check the labels of the gravy and malt vinegar if cooking gluten-free and find an alternative if needed.

BUDGET HACK: Choose one sauce rather than two.

2KG (4LB 8OZ) MARIS PIPER POTATOES
2 TSP CAYENNE PEPPER
1 SMALL ONION
1 HEAPED TBSP BISTO GRAVY
500ML (17FL OZ) VEGETABLE STOCK
1 TBSP MALT VINEGAR
2 TBSP CURRY POWDER
1 TBSP MANGO CHUTNEY
1 TBSP CORNFLOUR
100G (3½OZ) MOZZARELLA, GRATED
100G (3½OZ) EXTRA MATURE CHEDDAR
    CHEESE, GRATED
OLIVE OIL
SALT

01 Preheat your oven to 220°C/200°C fan/gas mark 7.

02 Fill a large bowl with cold water. Leaving the skin on, cut the potatoes into chunky chips, adding them to the bowl of water as you go.

03 Give the chips a good ruffle – this helps remove starch and makes them extra crispy. Drain them into a large saucepan. Cover with cold water, season with salt and bring to the boil. Once boiling, cook for 2 minutes (set a timer) then drain in a colander and leave to steam-dry.

04 Divide the chips between two large baking trays and drizzle with a good glug of olive oil. Season with salt and cayenne pepper. Toss together so that each chip is nicely coated then spread out into a single layer – the more space there is around each chip the crispier they will become. Roast in the oven for 40–45 minutes, turning halfway, until deep golden brown.

05 Meanwhile, make the sauces. For the gravy, peel and finely chop the onion. Get a saucepan over a low heat and drizzle in a little oil. Scrape in the onion and fry until soft. Add the gravy and 250ml (9fl oz) of the vegetable stock. Whisk well, season with ½ tablespoon of malt vinegar and keep warm.

06 Curry sauce time. Get a small saucepan over a low heat, drizzle in a splash of oil along with the curry powder. Cook, stirring for 30 seconds, then pour in the remaining vegetable stock. Add the mango chutney and remaining malt vinegar. In a small bowl, mix the cornflour into a milky paste with 1 tablespoon of water then pour into the curry sauce. Bubble away until thickened then keep warm.

07 Pile all the chips onto one baking tray. Preheat your grill to high. Sprinkle the grated cheese over the chips. Slide under the hot grill until the cheese has melted and is bubbling and golden. Serve at the table with the curry sauce and gravy for people to help themselves.

THE STICKIEST WINGS

GF, DF · ⏱ 50 MINS · SERVES 4

A popular Chinese dish from the '90s that we're bringing back with style. Unlike most wing recipes, these are cooked on the hob with the Coca-Cola reducing down to make the stickiest caramelized sauce. Make sure to use full-fat coke as you need those essential sugars.

GLUTEN-FREE: If you're cooking gluten-free, substitute the soy sauce for tamari.

BUDGET HACK: Leave out the Shaoxing wine/sherry.

1.2KG (2LB 12OZ) CHICKEN WINGS
THUMB-SIZED PIECE OF FRESH GINGER
2 TSP CHILLI FLAKES
500ML (17FL OZ) COCA-COLA
2 TBSP SOY SAUCE
2 TBSP SHAOXING WINE OR DRY
   SHERRY
2 SPRING ONIONS
NEUTRAL OIL, SUCH AS VEGETABLE,
   SUNFLOWER OR GROUNDNUT
SALT AND BLACK PEPPER

YOU WILL ALSO NEED KITCHEN PAPER.

01   Cut the chicken wings in half at the joint then pat dry with kitchen paper. Season with salt and black pepper. Thickly slice the ginger, leaving the skin on.

02   Get a large wok or frying pan over a high heat. Drizzle in a good glug of neutral oil. Add the chicken wings and fry for around 15 minutes, flipping regularly, until evenly browned. Add the ginger and chilli flakes to the pan. Stir and cook for a further 30 seconds.

03   Pour in the Coca-Cola, soy sauce and Shaoxing wine or sherry and give everything a good mix. Bring to the boil then cover the pan with a lid (or baking tray) and lower the heat to medium. Leave the chicken wings to simmer away for 15 minutes, then remove the lid and turn the heat back up to high.

04   Cook for a further 15 minutes until most of the sauce has evaporated and the wings are sticky and tender.

05   Give everything one final stir then pile onto a large serving plate. Thinly slice the spring onions (green and white parts) and scatter over the top. Serve at the table for people to help themselves.

SUPER STEAK SANDWICH

DF · ⏱ 30 MINS · SERVES 4

We've gone punchy with this one. Caramelized strips of
tender steak and gnarly fried courgettes are slathered with red
chimichurri and draped on a bed of rocket, mayo, and warm ciabatta.
That bright Argentinian condiment of roasted red peppers, chilli,
smoked paprika and vinegar is a big flavour win. Throw it in
all your sandwiches from here on in.

BUDGET HACK: Use a lesser-known cut of steak like bavette instead.

2 LOAVES CIABATTA
→ HEAD TO PAGE 140 TO MAKE YOUR OWN
4 ROASTED JARRED RED PEPPERS
2 RED CHILLIES
1 LARGE BUNCH OF FRESH CORIANDER
1 TSP SMOKED PAPRIKA
4 TBSP RED WINE VINEGAR
2 COURGETTES
2 SIRLOIN STEAKS
4 TBSP MAYONNAISE
1 SMALL BAG OF ROCKET
OLIVE OIL
SALT AND BLACK PEPPER

01 Heat the ciabatta loaves in a low oven, 120°C/100°C fan/gas mark ½.

02 Red chimichurri time. Finely chop the roasted peppers, chillies and coriander (stalks and all). Scrape into a bowl, then add the smoked paprika, red wine vinegar and 2 tablespoons of olive oil. Season to taste with salt and black pepper. Set aside.

03 Get a large griddle pan over a high heat and wait until it is searing hot, this will take a couple of minutes.

04 Meanwhile, thinly slice the courgettes. Season the steaks generously with salt and black pepper. Drizzle some olive oil into the hot frying pan. Add the steaks and fry for 2–2½ minutes on each side depending on thickness for medium–rare. Transfer them to a plate and leave to rest.

05 Add the courgettes to the pan (don't wash it up in between as you want all that steak flavour). Fry for 5 minutes, turning halfway until nicely charred. Remove from the heat.

06 Get the ciabatta out the oven. Cut into four and slice in half. Spread the bottom halves with mayonnaise. Slice the steaks into strips. Top the ciabatta bases with the steak, courgette and rocket then spoon over the red chimichurri to taste. Add the top halves of the ciabatta. Big win.

MOB CIABATTA

DF, VG · 🕐 4 HRS 30 MINS + OVERNIGHT FERMENTATION · MAKES 2 LOAVES

A bread for the more adventurous bakers out there because of how
finnicky it is to work with. Despite how difficult it makes things, the
sticky dough is what gives the ciabatta its airy pockets. So, bear with it.
Follow the recipe to a t and you won't be disappointed.

FOR THE BIGA
180G (6½OZ) STRONG WHITE BREAD
    FLOUR
115ML (3¾FL OZ) WARM WATER
A LARGE PINCH OF DRIED INSTANT
    YEAST

FOR THE DOUGH
275G (9¾OZ) STRONG WHITE BREAD
    FLOUR
250ML (9FL OZ) WARM WATER
3 TBSP EXTRA-VIRGIN OLIVE OIL
1¼ TSP DRIED INSTANT YEAST
1 TSP SALT

YOU WILL ALSO NEED BAKING PAPER.

01   The night before you want to make your ciabatta, make the overnight biga. Tip the flour, warm water and yeast into a bowl and mix really well until no lumps of flour remain. Cover with cling film with a small hole poked into it and leave for 12 hours.

02   The next day make the dough. Tip the flour, warm water, oil, yeast, salt and overnight biga into a large bowl and use clean hands to mix everything together until fully incorporated. It'll feel like a scarily wet dough MOB but stick with it!

03   Leave for 30 minutes covered with the cling flim then wet your hands and pick up a corner of the dough, stretch it up without ripping it and fold it towards you, up and over the dough. Repeat with the other three corners, wetting your hands each time. You should feel the dough tighten up a little as you go. Repeat this every 30 minutes for another 1 hour, then leave the dough to prove for a further 1½ hours untouched (so 3 hours in total).

04   Get a rectangular baking tray (roughly 20 × 30cm/8 × 12in) with a slight lip ready and cut two large, long strips of baking paper, flour them.

05   Tip the dough out onto a heavily floured work surface (this dough can be a sticky beast) and flour the top. Shape into a rough square using clean floured hands, then use a knife or dough scraper to cut into two rough rectangles – don't worry if they're not perfect. Carefully place each onto the pieces of baking paper and lift onto the tray, placing the loaves alongside each other – this will help them keep their shape. Don't be too rough with the dough, you want to keep all those bubbles and air.

06   Leave for 1 hour to prove.

07   Heat the oven to 220°C/200°C fan/gas mark 7 and put a heavy baking sheet or pizza stone in to heat up for at least 30 minutes.

08   When ready to bake, lightly flour the baking sheet or stone, then carefully flip each ciabatta onto it. Repeat with the other loaf then bang in the oven for 20 minutes until golden brown and hollow when tapped on the bottom.

09   Cool on a wire rack then serve with oil and vinegar for dipping.

01 Tip your biga, warm water, flour, oil and salt into a large bowl.

02 Mix to form your dough, it will feel extremely wet.

05 Tip your dough out on to a heavily floured work surface.

06 Shape into a square using clean floured hands.

03 Start to stretch and fold the dough.

04 Flour your surface.

07 Cut into two long rectangles.

08 Place on a baking tray and prove for an hour before baking.

MUSHROOM & TALEGGIO GNOCCHI BAKE

V · ⏱ 30 MINS · SERVES 4

A delicious, warming bake that diehard MOB fans will already know and love from our website. The creamy-savoury combination of Taleggio and mushrooms takes the gnocchi to the next level.

VEGGIE: Check the label of the Taleggio cheese if cooking veggie and find an alternative if needed.

BUDGET HACK: Use the same amount of button mushrooms instead of the mixed packet.

200G (7OZ) PACKET OF MIXED
    MUSHROOMS
250G (9OZ) CHESTNUT MUSHROOMS
1 BUNCH OF FRESH PARSLEY, PLUS
    EXTRA FOR GARNISHING
1 GARLIC CLOVE
A SMALL HANDFUL OF FRESH THYME
2 TSP CHILLI FLAKES
½ LEMON
4 TBSP SINGLE CREAM
150G (5½OZ) BABY LEAF SPINACH
800G (1LB 12OZ) GNOCCHI
100G (3½OZ) TALEGGIO CHEESE
OLIVE OIL
SALT AND BLACK PEPPER

01 Slice the mushrooms and roughly chop the parsley. Get a large frying pan over a high heat and drizzle in some olive oil. Chuck in the mushrooms and fry until browned and shrivelled.

02 Peel and crush in the garlic clove, add the thyme leaves, 1 teaspoon of chilli flakes, a handful of chopped parsley and finely grate in the lemon zest. Mix everything in.

03 Pour in the single cream and allow it to bubble away by half. Then add the spinach and leave it to wilt.

04 Add the gnocchi to a bowl, cover with boiling water and leave for 5 minutes.

05 Back to your sauce. Once the spinach has wilted, squeeze in the lemon juice.

06 Mix in 3 tablespoons of water from the gnocchi bowl to the sauce. Drain the gnocchi in a sieve or a colander. Add to the sauce and give everything a good mix together. Season well with salt and black pepper.

07 Preheat your grill to high.

08 Pour the gnocchi into a medium-sized baking dish. Slice the Taleggio and place on top of the gnocchi. Sprinkle over the remaining chilli flakes and place under the grill for 5–8 minutes, until golden and bubbling.

09 Spoon the gnocchi into four bowls, top with some more chopped parsley to serve and tuck in.

AUBERGINE PARMIGIANA SUB

V · ⏱ 40 MINS · SERVES 4

What's better than an aubergine parm? An aubergine parm
that's been lovingly wedged in a soft sub roll. There is a small Italian
deli called Fine Food's, opposite our first studio in Bermondsey.
Their tip with parmigiana was to salt and then flour the aubergine
before it's fried – it makes them meltingly tender and
super-crisp without soaking up too much oil.

VEGGIE: Check the label of the Parmesan and mozzarella cheese if cooking veggie and find an alternative if needed.

BUDGET HACK: Use pre-grated mozzarella.

2 AUBERGINES

1 ONION

2 FAT GARLIC CLOVES

½ TSP DRIED CHILLI FLAKES

1 × 400G (14OZ) TIN OF PLUM
    TOMATOES

1 TSP CASTER SUGAR

4 TBSP PLAIN FLOUR

4 LARGE SUB ROLLS

A HANDFUL OF FRESH BASIL LEAVES

2 × 125G (4½OZ) BALLS OF
    MOZZARELLA

50G (1¾OZ) PARMESAN CHEESE

OLIVE OIL

SALT AND BLACK PEPPER

01 Trim the ends off the aubergines then cut lengthways into 1cm (½in)-long strips. Season with salt and leave for 20 minutes whilst you make the sauce.

02 Peel and finely chop the onion and garlic cloves. Get a small saucepan over a medium heat. Drizzle in a good glug of olive oil. Scrape in the onion along with a pinch of salt and fry, stirring occasionally, until completely soft. Add the garlic and chilli flakes and fry, stirring for 30 seconds, then tip in the tin of plum tomatoes. Use the back of your spoon to break up the tomatoes, add the sugar then lower the heat and leave the sauce to simmer away.

03 Spoon the flour out onto a plate. Lightly coat half the aubergine slices in the flour – this will help make them jammy and soft without absorbing too much oil. Get a large non-stick frying pan over a medium–high heat, drizzle in a good amount of oil then place half the floured aubergine slices in the pan. Fry for 6–8 minutes, turning halfway, until golden and soft. Transfer to a plate then repeat with the remaining aubergine.

04 Preheat your grill to high. Slice the rolls three-quarters of the way through the centre, opening them up slightly so you can fit in the most amount of filling. Season your sauce with salt and black pepper and stir through most of the basil leaves.

05 Assembly time. Thinly spread sauce over the bottom of each sub. Layer up the aubergine, more sauce and mozzarella, tearing the cheese in as you go, making sure to finish with a layer of mozzarella. Finely grate over the Parmesan. Season with black pepper then slide under the hot grill until golden and bubbling. Tear over the remaining basil leaves and drizzle with a little more oil to serve.

ALL THE CHEESY GREENS

V · ⏱ 45 MINS · SERVES 4

We see your cauliflower cheese, and we raise you all the cheesy greens. Charred, roasted wedges of cabbage and broccoli, handfuls of sweet peas, and bushels of kale are coated in the cheesiest sauce imaginable and cooked until bubbling and golden. Serve with garlic bread and a fat mustardy salad. Yes.

VEGGIE: Check the label of the Cheddar or Gruyère cheese if cooking veggie and find an alternative if needed.

BUDGET HACK: Use just Cheddar cheese in the sauce.

1 POINTED (SWEETHEART) CABBAGE
1 LARGE BROCCOLI HEAD
75G (2¾OZ) BUTTER
75G (2¾OZ) PLAIN FLOUR
750ML (1¼ PINTS) WHOLE MILK
200G (7OZ) OF YOUR FAVOURITE
    HARD CHEESE → (WE LIKE A MIX
    OF EXTRA-MATURE CHEDDAR AND
    GRUYÈRE CHEESE)
1 TBSP DIJON MUSTARD
200G (7OZ) FROZEN PEAS
4 LARGE HANDFULS OF KALE
2 TBSP WHITE WINE VINEGAR
2 CHICORY OR 1 ROMAINE LETTUCE
    HEART
OLIVE OIL
SALT AND BLACK PEPPER
GARLIC BREAD, TO SERVE

01   Preheat your oven to 220°C/200°C fan/gas mark 7.

02   Cut the cabbage and broccoli into four wedges each. Keep the stalk on the broccoli (it's the best bit). Spread out into a medium high-sided roasting tin or baking dish. Drizzle with a good amount of olive oil and season with salt and black pepper. Roast in the oven for 15 minutes.

03   Meanwhile, make the cheese sauce. Get a medium saucepan over a medium heat. Add the butter and let it melt. Stir in the flour and cook for 1 minute. Gradually pour in the milk, whisking as you go to keep the sauce lump-free. Bubble away for 5 minutes, stirring, until thickened. Grate in three-quarters of the cheese. Once melted add 1 teaspoon of the mustard and season with salt and black pepper.

04   Tip the frozen peas into the roasting tin, scatter over the kale then pour over the cheese sauce. Grate the remaining cheese on top. Bake in the oven for 20–25 minutes until bubbling and golden brown.

05   Salad time. Whisk the remaining mustard and white wine vinegar together in a bowl with 4 tablespoons of olive oil to create a dressing. Season to taste with salt and black pepper. Slice the lettuce and mix everything together in the bowl.

06   Serve the cheesy greens out of the pan with the salad and some garlic bread for people to help themselves

FRIED MOZZARELLA SANDWICH WITH TOMATO & CAPER RELISH

V · ⏱ 25 MINS · SERVES 4

This recipe is so good and painfully simple. It is the Italians we need to thank for the genius idea of frying breaded mozzarella and slinging it between a couple of slices of bread, but we've put our own spin on this sando. To cut through the richness, we've added a tangy, chilli-spiked relish. It's sublime.

VEGGIE: Check the label of the mozzarella if cooking veggie and find an alternative if needed.

BUDGET HACK: To be honest MOB, this one's pretty cheap already!

1 RED ONION
1 SMALL BUNCH OF FRESH PARSLEY
2 LARGE RIPE TOMATOES
2 TBSP CAPERS
BIG PINCH CHILLI FLAKES
2 TBSP RED WINE VINEGAR
8 SLICES OF WHITE BREAD
2 × 125G (4½OZ) MOZZARELLA BALLS
6 TBSP PLAIN FLOUR
2 LARGE EGGS
100G (3½-OZ) PANKO BREADCRUMBS
OLIVE OIL
VEGETABLE OIL
SALT AND BLACK PEPPER
SALAD AND/OR OVEN FRENCH FRIES,
    TO SERVE

YOU WILL ALSO NEED KITCHEN PAPER.

01   Relish time. Peel and finely chop the red onion and parsley. Cut the tomatoes into a similar size as the capers. Scrape into a bowl, mix in the capers, chilli flakes, red wine vinegar and 2 tablespoons of olive oil, and add some salt and black pepper to season. You want the relish to be tangy to cut through the mozzarella sandwich. Set aside.

02   Cut all the crusts off the bread. Slice the mozzarella into thick rounds. Divide the sliced mozzarella between four slices of bread, then top with the remaining bread slices.

03   Get out three bowls. Spoon the flour into one and season with salt and black pepper. Crack and whisk the eggs into another and tip the breadcrumbs into the final bowl.

04   Working one at a time, coat each sandwich first in a thin layer of flour, then in the egg. Finally encase completely in the breadcrumbs, making sure that the sides of the sandwiches are well sealed. Place onto a baking tray.

05   Get a large frying pan over a high heat. Pour in enough vegetable oil to just coat the bottom of the pan and heat until shimmering. In two batches, fry the sandwiches for 1–2 minutes on each side until crisp and golden. Drain on kitchen paper and season with salt.

06   Cut the sandwiches in half. Serve with the tomato and caper relish and some salad and/or fries.

ORZO CACIO E PEPE-ISH

V · ⏱ 15 MINS · SERVES 4

If there's one recipe that you are going to cook time and time again, it's this. We have nailed the cheesy, creamy pepperiness of an authentic cacio e pepe, and this is the easiest version of that dish in existence. Everything's cooked in one pan and the orzo pasta water automatically emulsifies the sauce. It couldn't get any better.

VEGGIE: Check the label of the Parmesan cheese if cooking veggie and find an alternative if needed.

BUDGET HACK: MOB, trust us with this one, do not change a thing.

400G (14OZ) DRIED ORZO PASTA
100G (3½OZ) PARMESAN CHEESE
1 TBSP BLACK PEPPERCORNS
100G (3½OZ) BUTTER
1 LEMON
SALT

01   Measure 750ml (1¼ pints) of water into a large saucepan. Bring to the boil and season with salt. Drop in the orzo pasta. Cook for 7–8 minutes, until you are left with around 100ml (3½fl oz) of water and the orzo pasta is nearly cooked.

02   Meanwhile, finely grate the Parmesan cheese onto a chopping board. Crush the peppercorns, and then toast them in a pan with no oil, until they start smoking.

03   Once the orzo is ready, lower the heat to medium and stir in the butter. Once melted, stir in the Parmesan in three additions, waiting for the first to melt before adding the next one. Once all the Parmesan has been added you should be left with a silky, glossy sauce. Add a splash more water if the sauce looks a little thick.

04   Stir through the cracked toasted black pepper and finely grate in the lemon zest. Spoon the orzo into four bowls. Heaven.

5

IMPRESSIVE

Comfort dishes for
when you've got your MOB over
– these will steal the show.

SALT & PEPPER CRAB CAKES

DF · ○ 35 MINS · SERVES 3

These delicate black pepper, ginger, coriander and lime crab cakes make for an unreal starter. We've fried spring onions and chilli for a fiery garnish that looks just as good as it tastes. Serve these to anyone you want to impress. You can also serve them with our Stickiest Wings (see page 132) for the most epic start to a meal.

BUDGET HACK: Use tinned crab meat instead.

1 BUNCH OF SPRING ONIONS

1 SMALL BUNCH OF FRESH CORIANDER

THUMB-SIZED PIECE OF FRESH GINGER

2 GARLIC CLOVES

1 LIME

200G (7OZ) MIXED BROWN AND WHITE
    CRAB MEAT

50G (1¾OZ) PANKO BREADCRUMBS

1 TBSP FISH SAUCE

1 LARGE EGG

1 TBSP BLACK PEPPER

2 TBSP CORNFLOUR

2 RED CHILLIES

NEUTRAL OIL, SUCH AS VEGETABLE,
    SUNFLOWER OR GROUNDNUT

SALT

SWEET CHILLI SAUCE AND/OR
    MAYONNAISE, TO SERVE

01 Thinly slice half of the spring onions (green and white parts). Finely chop the coriander stalks (reserving the leaves). Scrape into a large bowl.

02 Peel and finely grate the ginger and garlic cloves into the bowl, then grate in the lime zest. Add the crab meat, breadcrumbs and fish sauce. Crack in the egg and most of the black pepper. Season with salt then mix together well to combine. Form into nine patties with your hands and set aside on a plate.

03 Spoon the cornflour onto a separate plate. Mix in the remaining black pepper as well as a good pinch of salt. Thickly slice the remaining spring onions and red chillies on a diagonal. Roughly chop the coriander leaves and cut the lime into wedges.

04 Get a large non-stick frying pan over a medium–high heat and drizzle in a good glug of neutral oil. Pat the crab cakes on both sides in the cornflour mixture. Place in the pan and fry for 2–3 minutes on each side until crisp and golden brown.

05 Divide the crab cakes between three plates. Put the frying pan back over a high heat. Drizzle in a splash more oil and add the spring onion and chillies to the pan. Fry for 2–3 minutes until softened and lightly charred, then spoon over the crab cakes. Add a lime wedge to each bowl, scatter over the coriander and serve with sweet chilli sauce/ mayo for dipping.

ASPARAGUS BENEDICT WITH CHIPOTLE HOLLANDAISE

V · ⏱ 35 MINS · SERVES 4

If you've never made your own hollandaise, this recipe is for you. If you have made your own hollandaise, then this is still the recipe for you. Because this chipotle-spiked sauce will trump whatever you've made before. See just how easy it is to make this decadent brunch dish by putting a fruity, smoky spin on the rich French sauce.

BUDGET HACK: This one is good as it is.

140G (5OZ) BUTTER
6 LARGE EGGS
2 TSP WHITE WINE VINEGAR
3 TSP CHIPOTLE PASTE
½ LEMON
400G (14OZ) ASPARAGUS SPEARS
4 MUFFINS
OLIVE OIL
SALT AND BLACK PEPPER

YOU WILL ALSO NEED KITCHEN PAPER.

01   Get a small saucepan over a medium heat. Add the butter and let it melt. Once melted, set aside. Fill a separate small saucepan a third of the way full with water, put over a low heat and bring to a low simmer.

02   Separate two of the eggs (freeze the egg whites to be used another time), and put the yolks into a glass bowl (size-wise it needs to fit nicely over the saucepan of water). Add 1 teaspoon of the white wine vinegar and 1 tablespoon of cold water.

03   Sit the bowl over the just-simmering water and whisk. Keep whisking for 3–5 minutes until the egg yolks have turned paler in colour and almost doubled in size. Take the bowl off the heat, and whilst whisking, gradually pour in the melted butter. Go slow and steady here, waiting for the first bit of butter to be incorporated before you add the next – this will stop you splitting the hollandaise.

04   Once all the butter has been added, whisk in the chipotle paste. Season with salt, black pepper and lemon juice to taste. Hollandaise done. Set aside and keep warm.

05   Put your oven on a low heat, 120°C/100°C fan/gas mark ½.

06   Pour the water from the saucepan into a larger pan, top up with more water and salt, and bring to the boil. Snap the woody ends off the asparagus then drop into the boiling water. Cook for 1–2 minutes until just tender then remove with a slotted spoon onto a baking tray. Drizzle with a little olive oil, season with salt and black pepper and keep warm in the oven.

07   Slice the muffins in half and toast. Keep warm in the oven along with the asparagus.

08   Poached egg time. Pour the remaining vinegar into the saucepan, control the heat so that the water is at a rolling boil. Use the top of your spoon to create a whirlpool effect. Crack two of your eggs into the pan, as close to the water as possible. Cook for 3–4 minutes until the white is set and the yolk is still runny. Drain with a slotted spoon onto kitchen paper. Repeat with the remaining eggs.

09   Divide the muffins between four plates. Top with the asparagus and poached eggs and spoon over the chipotle hollandaise to serve.

CELERIAC SCHNITZEL

V · ⏱ 50 MINS · SERVES 4

Welcome to the wonderful world of celeriac. Don't be scared by the veg's gnarly, knobbled exterior as its flesh is sweet, nutty and uncannily meat-like when roasted. Here we've breaded and fried it for a veggie take on a classic schnitzel. The caper and shallot dressing is killer.

VEGGIE: Check the label of the Pecorino or Parmesan cheese if cooking veggie and find an alternative if needed.

BUDGET HACK: Swap the hazelnuts for pumpkin seeds.

1 LARGE CELERIAC
50G (1¾OZ) HAZELNUTS
1 BANANA SHALLOT
1 SMALL HANDFUL OF FRESH DILL
2 TBSP CAPERS
2 TSP DIJON OR WHOLEGRAIN
    MUSTARD
2 TBSP APPLE CIDER OR WHITE WINE
    VINEGAR
1 APPLE
6 TBSP PLAIN FLOUR
2 EGGS
75G (2¾OZ) PANKO BREADCRUMBS
1 LARGE BAG OF WATERCRESS
OLIVE OIL
VEGETABLE OIL
SALT AND BLACK PEPPER
PECORINO OR PARMESAN CHEESE, TO
    SERVE

YOU WILL ALSO NEED KITCHEN PAPER.

01   Preheat your oven to 200°C/180°C fan/gas mark 6.

02   Peel the celeriac, trim off the ends and cut into four steaks, around 1½cm (⅝in) in thickness. Cut the trimmed ends into smallish cubes.

03   Lay the steaks and cubed celeriac out onto a baking tray, drizzle with a little olive oil and season with salt and black pepper. Roast the steaks in the oven for 20 minutes until partially cooked through, remove onto a plate and set aside. Keep the celeriac cubes in the oven for a further 15 minutes until cooked through. Add the hazelnuts to the tray for the last 5 minutes so that they get a nice toast. Leave to cool.

04   Vinaigrette time. Peel the shallot, finely chop the shallot and dill, scrape into a bowl. Add the capers, mustard, vinegar and 3 tablespoons of olive oil. Season to taste with salt and black pepper. Roughly chop the hazelnuts and cut the apple into smallish cubes.

05   Get out three bowls. Spoon the flour into one and season with salt and black pepper. Crack and whisk the eggs in another and tip the breadcrumbs into the final bowl.

06   One by one, coat the celeriac steaks in the flour, then the eggs and then finally in the breadcrumbs – at this point they will begin to look like a schnitzel.

07   Get a large frying pan over a high heat. Drizzle in enough vegetable oil to coat the bottom of the pan by 1cm (½in). Heat until shimmering. Fry the celeriac schnitzel in two batches for 1–2 minutes on each side until deeply golden. Drain on kitchen paper.

08   Pile the watercress onto four plates, scatter over the celeriac cubes, apple and hazelnuts. Lay a schnitzel on top then spoon over the vinaigrette. Top with shavings of Pecorino or Parmesan cheese, to serve.

SLOW-COOKED PORK BELLY WITH APPLE & CIDER GRAVY & ROAST GARLIC MASH

GF · ⏱ 3 HRS + RESTING MEAT OVERNIGHT · SERVES 4

Everyone knows the best thing about pork is the crackling and we've nailed it here, thanks to a few clever tricks. The pork slow-cooks with onion, apple, and cider to create its own gravy while the skin on top gets Earth-shatteringly crisp. The roast garlic mash? A strike of genius.

BUDGET HACK: Use a cheap cider instead, although the gravy will be sweeter.

1.5KG (3LB 5OZ) BONELESS PORK BELLY JOINT

2 ONIONS

1 LARGE GARLIC BULB

300ML (10½FL OZ) CHICKEN STOCK

500ML (17FL OZ) BOTTLE OF DRY CIDER

3 APPLES

800G (1LB 12OZ) POTATOES

100G (3½ OZ) BUTTER

1 TBSP WHOLEGRAIN MUSTARD

OLIVE OIL

SALT AND BLACK PEPPER

STEAMED GREENS, TO SERVE (OPTIONAL)

YOU WILL ALSO NEED KITCHEN PAPER.

01   The night before, score the pork belly by making 12–14 diagonal cuts through the skin, being careful not to cut the meat. Place the pork skin-side up onto a wire tray over a roasting tin. Boil a kettle then pour the water over the skin. Drain the water then pat the pork dry with kitchen paper. Put on a plate, uncovered, in the fridge to dry out overnight.

02   The next day, preheat your oven to 220°C/200°C fan/gas mark 7. Get the pork out of the fridge to come up to room temperature, lightly rub the skin with olive oil and season all over with salt and black pepper. Peel the onions and cut them into thick slices.

03   Lay the onions in the bottom of a high-sided roasting tin. Place the pork, skin-side up, on top and roast in the oven for 30 minutes.

04   Reduce the heat to 160°C/140°C fan/gas mark 3. Nestle the garlic bulb into the roasting tin. Pour the stock and cider in around the meat, – careful not to get any liquid on the skin. Roast for a further 1½ hours.

05   Core and cut each apple into eight wedges. Chuck them into the roasting tin then remove the garlic bulb and set aside. Roast the pork for a further 30 minutes until the crackling is crisp and the meat meltingly tender. To make crispier crackling, slide under the grill for a few minutes.

06   Meanwhile, mash time. Peel the potatoes and cut into quarters. Tip into a large saucepan of cold salted water and bring to the boil. Cook until mashable, about 10–15 minutes, drain in a colander and steam-dry for a few minutes. Tip back into the saucepan. Squeeze the garlic out of its skin by pressing a knife down on it and add in. Add the butter, then mash together and season with salt and black pepper to taste. Keep warm.

07   Come back to the pork. Remove from the oven, transfer it to a plate and leave to rest. Pour the gravy through a sieve into a small saucepan. Tip all of the apples and onions onto the same plate as the pork.

08   Get the gravy over a high heat and bubble away for 10 minutes until reduced slightly, skimming off any noticeable fat. Whisk the mustard into the gravy, then tip back in the apples and onions and season with salt and black pepper.

09   Cut the pork into four. Dollop the mash onto four plates, add the pork and spoon over the gravy along with the apple and onions. Serve with some steamed greens if you like.

BEETROOT & VODKA-CURED SALMON BAGEL STATION

⏱ 30 MINS + 24 HRS CURING · SERVES 4 WITH LEFTOVER SALMON

Making your own salmon gravlax couldn't be simpler, or more impressive. All you need to do is mix together a cure, cover the salmon adequately, and then let it sit for 24 hours. We've used beetroot as we love the bright and vibrant colour it brings. Once you've tried this, you'll never buy smoked salmon again.

BUDGET HACK: No need to pimp the cream cheese, keep it simple and let the salmon speak for itself.

2 TBSP CORIANDER SEEDS
300G (10½OZ) RAW BEETROOT
120G (4¼OZ) COARSE SEA SALT
80G (2¾OZ) CASTER SUGAR
2 LEMONS
50ML (1¾FL OZ) VODKA
1KG (2LB 4OZ) SIDE OF SALMON, SKIN ON → GET THIS FROM A FISHMONGER AND ASK THEM TO PIN BONE IT FOR YOU
4 PICKLED CORNICHONS
180G (6½OZ) CREAM CHEESE
1 TBSP HORSERADISH
A HANDFUL OF FRESH CHIVES
4 BAGELS OF YOUR CHOICE
SALT AND BLACK PEPPER

01   Toast the coriander seeds in a dry frying pan over a medium heat until smelling great. Set aside to cool.

02   Give the beetroot a good scrub then leaving the skin on coarsely grate into a large bowl – this will temporarily stain your hands so wear gloves if you like! Add the salt, sugar and coriander seeds. Finely grate in the lemon zest, pour in the vodka and mix to combine.

03   Stretch a large double layer of cling film, big enough to encase the salmon, over the work surface. Spoon a third of the cure into the centre and lay the salmon, skin-side down, on top. Pack the rest of the beetroot cure over the top and sides of the salmon then wrap tightly in cling film.

04   Place onto a baking tray. Put in the fridge for 24 hours, flipping the salmon occasionally so it stays evenly coated in the cure. Don't worry about the liquid that collects in the bottom of the tray, that's normal.

05   Once cured, unwrap the salmon, scrape off the beetroot mixture and rinse the fish thoroughly under cold water. Pat dry. The salmon is now ready to be thinly sliced and can be kept in a tupperware in the fridge for up to a week.

06   Bagel time. Finely chop the cornichons and scrape into a bowl. Combine the cream cheese with the horseradish, then place in the bowl, snip in the chives then mix together and season to taste with salt and black pepper. Toast the bagels. Cut a lemon into wedges and serve with the salmon.

ROASTED GARLIC & RICOTTA RAVIOLI WITH CONFIT TOMATOES

V · 🕐 3 HRS · SERVES 4

VEGGIE: Check the label of the Parmesan cheese if cooking veggie and find an alternative if needed.

BUDGET HACK: Substitute the pine nuts for pumpkin seeds.

TIP: Freeze any remaining ravioli and cook from frozen in 3–4 minutes for a super-quick meal!

Keep the leftover confit tomato oil in a jar for up to a month and use on everything!

FOR THE PASTA DOUGH
300G (10½OZ) '00' FLOUR (THIS GIVES
    THE PASTA ITS COLOUR AND
    ELASTICITY)
3 LARGE EGGS

600G (1LB 5OZ) CHERRY TOMATOES
1 GARLIC BULB
1 TSP CHILLI FLAKES
400ML (14FL OZ) OLIVE OIL
250G (9OZ) RICOTTA CHEESE
1 LEMON
50G (1¾OZ) PARMESAN CHEESE, PLUS
    EXTRA TO SERVE
'00' FLOUR, FOR DUSTING
50G (1¾OZ) TOASTED PINE NUTS
A HANDFUL OF BASIL LEAVES
SALT AND BLACK PEPPER

YOU WILL ALSO NEED A FOOD
PROCESSOR AND A PASTA MACHINE.

Ravioli are little parcels of happiness, and this recipe proves you don't have to be an Italian nonna to make them. Our fail-safe dough is super-easy and can be scaled up or down. Slow-roasted tomatoes provide a sweet ballast to the smooth ricotta filling.

01   To make your pasta dough, blitz the flour and eggs together in a food processor until just coming together to form a shaggy dough.

02   Tip out onto your work surface and knead together until fairly stiff yet still pliable. If it feels super soft, knead in a little flour and if you are forcing it to come together sprinkle over a little water as you go. Keep kneading for 5 minutes until nice and smooth. Wrap in cling film and leave to rest in the fridge for at least 30 minutes before using or until ready to use. Well covered, the dough can be left overnight.

03   Preheat your oven to 150°C/130°C fan/gas mark 2.

04   Tip the cherry tomatoes and garlic bulb into a small roasting tin – you want them to be tightly packed so that when you pour over the olive oil they will be submerged. Season well with salt and black pepper, sprinkle over the chilli flakes then pour over the oil. Roast in the oven for 1–1 hour 30 minutes until the garlic is completely soft and the tomatoes have shrivelled but not burst. Set aside to cool then drain the oil from the tomatoes and garlic, keeping both the vegetables and the oil.

05   For the ravioli filling, squeeze the garlic from its skin by pressing a knife down on it. Add to a bowl with the ricotta then finely grate in the lemon zest and Parmesan. Season with salt, black pepper and lemon juice to taste.

06   Pasta time. Set your pasta machine up onto the widest setting. Grab your rested dough from the fridge and cut into four pieces. Place three pieces aside and cover with a clean tea towel. Flatten the quarter of dough into a rough rectangle with your hands then feed through the pasta machine on the widest setting.

07   Fold the pasta back over itself so that it is the same width as the pasta machine then roll it through again – this helps it become a smoother texture. Continue to feed the pasta through the machine, narrowing the setting each time until you get to the second thinnest setting. Place the long pasta sheet on a floured surface.

08   Spoon heaped teaspoons of the filling along the centre of the bottom length of the pasta sheet, leaving a 2½cm (1in) gap between each one. Use a little water on your finger to wet the pasta around the filling then fold over the top half to encase. Gently press down to make sure everything is sealed in. You want to make sure there is no room for air bubbles so that the ravioli stays tightly shut when cooked. Use a pizza cutter or sharp knife to cut into individual square ravioli. Transfer to two well-floured trays. Repeat with all the remaining pasta dough and filling. You should get around 7–8 ravioli from each sheet of pasta. *This is a great recipe to make with a mate, one of you on rolling and the other on shaping.*

09   Bring a large saucepan of salted water to the boil. Get your largest frying pan over a medium heat. Add the confit tomatoes, drizzle in a good glug of their oil and heat through.

10   Drop the ravioli into the boiling water. Cook for 2–3 minutes until they float then drain with a slotted spoon straight into the sauce. Carefully toss everything together, adding a good splash of pasta water to bring the sauce together. If your pan isn't big enough then do this in two batches.

11   Divide the ravioli between four bowls. Spoon over the sauce. Top with the pine nuts, basil leaves, a good grating of Parmesan and a drizzle more of tomato oil to serve.

SPATCHCOCK CHICKEN WITH POTATOES & SALSA VERDE

GF · ⏱ 1 HR 30 MINS · SERVES 4 · BY ELENA SILCOCK

Spatchcocking – welcome to the best way to cook a chicken. It's one of handiest tricks I have ever learned and I'll tell everyone about it forever. So the potatoes are gonna cook in the juices – steaming and getting more and more delicious by the minute, sizzling and crisping up in the chicken fat. THEN you're gonna serve it up with a sharp salsa verde. Yeah, you're welcome. P.S. Please buy a nice chicken, it's a treat and it's worth it.

BUDGET HACK: Choose just one large bunch of your favourite herb for the butter.

1.4KG–1.6KG (3LB 2OZ–3LB 8OZ) CHICKEN
2 GARLIC CLOVES
1 LEMON
50G SOFT BUTTER
2 TSP DRIED OREGANO
1KG (2LB 4OZ) POTATOES → I USE CHARLOTTE POTATOES HERE BUT YOU CAN CHOP UP MARIS PIPERS OR WHATEVER YOU FANCY
SMALL BUNCH OF PARSLEY, MINT AND DILL (YOU CAN GO FOR ANY HERBS HERE, I SWAP DEPENDING ON MY MOOD)
3 TBSP CAPERS
50G (1¾OZ) TIN OF ANCHOVY FILLETS IN OIL
1 TSP HONEY
1 TSP DIJON MUSTARD
OLIVE OIL
SALT AND BLACK PEPPER
SALAD OR GREEN VEG, TO SERVE (OPTIONAL)

YOU WILL ALSO NEED SCISSORS.

01 Take the chicken out of the fridge and let it sit for 15–30 mins so it comes up to room temp. Preheat your oven to 220°C/200°C fan/gas mark 7. First, let's spatchcock the chicken. You need some strong scissors. Turn the chicken breast-side down – you'll now be able to see the backbone of the chicken running up the middle of the bird. Use your scissors to cut from the neck to the cavity along each side of this bone, so you remove it completely.

02 Flip the chicken over so the breasts are now facing up, turn the wing bones upwards, and twist the thighs out so they both lie flat, then press down on the breastbone to flatten the chicken. You'll hear the wishbone break.

03 Peel the garlic. Grate the garlic and lemon zest into the butter, add the oregano and season generously with salt and pepper. Use your hands to separate the chicken skin from the meat – you can do this by sliding your finger under the skin and gently teasing it away from the meat. Then press two-thirds of the flavoured butter into the space you've created, using your hands to move it across the breast and over the thigh meat. Rub the remaining third over the outside of the bird. Season the outside of the chicken with salt and pepper. Place your chicken directly on an oven rack, and slide back into the oven near the top.

04 Grab your largest roasting tin and chuck the potatoes into it, season with salt and pepper, add a couple of tablespoons of water, then slide it under the rack with the chicken on it and roast everything for 35–40 mins (push to 45 minutes if your chicken is nearer to 1.6kg/3lb 8oz).

05 Squeeze the juice from the lemon. Make the salsa verde by blitzing the herbs, capers, anchovies, honey, mustard and lemon juice together with a splash of the oil. Once they're finely chopped, tip into a bowl and add enough olive oil to make it a drizzle-able consistency. Season well with salt and black pepper.

06 Slide the chicken out of the oven, it should be super-golden and crispy. Set aside on a plate to rest. Take the tin of potatoes (they should be sitting in a little liquid), and use a spatula or a back of the spoon or a spatula to smash them down into the juices, then return to the oven for 10–15 minutes more, until perfectly cooked and a little crispy around the edges. I usually use this time to make a salad or fry up some greens to go with.

07 Carve up the chicken and put onto a big plate. Serve alongside the crispy potatoes, salad or green veg if using, and drizzle on the salsa verde.

SLOW-COOKED SPICED LAMB SHOULDER, SLAW & ZHOUG

🕐 4 HRS 30 MINS · SERVES 4 WITH SOME LEFTOVERS

We first devised this as the ultimate hangover cure – it's the perfect
thing to whack in the oven and cook low and slow on a Sunday.
Meltingly soft lamb, zingy slaw, spicy zhoug and flatbreads. Beautiful.

BUDGET HACK: Use the same quantity of ras el hanout spice mix instead of all the dried spices.

1 TBSP SMOKED PAPRIKA

1 TBSP GROUND CORIANDER

2 TSP GROUND CINNAMON

1½ TBSP GROUND CUMIN, PLUS ½ TSP

2 RED ONIONS

1 BULB GARLIC

1 BONE-IN SHOULDER OF LAMB
   (APPROX. 1.5KG/3LB 5 OZ)

½ SMALL RED CABBAGE

2 CARROTS

2 YELLOW PEPPERS

1 TBSP DRIED MINT

1–2 TBSP RED WINE VINEGAR

SMALL BUNCH OF FRESH CORIANDER

1–2 GREEN CHILLIES (DEPENDING ON
   HOW SPICY YOU LIKE IT)

½ LEMON

8 LARGE FLATBREADS → IF YOU WANT
   TO MAKE YOUR OWN CHECK OUT
   OUR RECIPE FOR HUMMUS AND
   FLATBREADS ON PAGE 54

OLIVE OIL

SALT AND BLACK PEPPER

GREEK YOGHURT, TO SERVE

01   Preheat your oven to 170°C/150°C fan/gas mark 3.

02   Mix the smoked paprika, coriander, cinnamon and 1½ tablespoons of the cumin in a small bowl. Cut one and a half red onions into wedges. Take one clove of garlic out of the bulb and peel to be used later.

03   Rub the lamb all over with the spice mix and season with salt and black pepper. Transfer to a high-sided roasting tin along with the onion wedges and garlic bulb. Drizzle over olive oil then pour in enough water to submerge the bottom half of the meat. Cover the tray with a layer of baking paper and then foil. Make sure it's tightly sealed. Roast in the oven for 3½–4 hours until meltingly tender, it should shred with two forks.

04   Once the lamb is cooked, shred into the pan with the onions. Squeeze the garlic out from its skin and mix into the meat. Season with salt and black pepper then place back into the oven, uncovered, for the sauce to reduce while you make everything else.

05   Slaw and zhoug time. Thinly slice the remaining onion half and scrape into a large bowl. Finely shred or coarsely grate in the cabbage and carrots. Slice the peppers, add to the bowl along with the dried mint and 1 tablespoon of the red wine vinegar. Toss the slaw, season with salt and black pepper to taste, adding more vinegar if you like.

06   For the sauce, blitz the coriander (stalks and all) in a food processor with the green chilli, remaining garlic clove, cumin and a good drizzle of oil until a smooth, drizzling sauce. Add a splash of water to loosen if it needs it. Season with salt, black pepper and lemon juice to taste.

07   Heat the flatbreads. Remove the lamb from the oven and serve DIY style at the table with the warm flatbreads and slaw, zhoug and yoghurt for topping for the ultimate style kebabs.

PAN-FRIED COD WITH HAZELNUT ROMESCO & COURGETTES

GF, DF · ⏱ 50 MINS · SERVES 4

Hazelnuts, grilled peppers and a dash of smoky paprika make a next-level romesco sauce that really brings the best out of firm and flaky pan-fried cod. If you've never tried roasting Little Gem lettuce before, you're in for a treat. This is summer comfort food at its finest.

BUDGET HACK: Use sustainably sourced pollock instead.

2 RED PEPPERS
100G (3½ OZ) HAZELNUTS
3 COURGETTES
2 LITTLE GEM LETTUCES
1 SMALL CLOVE OF GARLIC
1 TBSP SHERRY OR RED WINE VINEGAR, PLUS A SPLASH FOR DRIZZLING
2 TSP SMOKED PAPRIKA
4 LARGE BONELESS SKINLESS COD FILLETS
A HANDFUL OF FRESH PARSLEY
1 LEMON
OLIVE OIL
SALT AND BLACK PEPPER

01 Preheat your grill to high.

02 Whack the whole peppers under the grill for around 15 minutes, turning occasionally until softened and nicely charred. Transfer to a bowl, cover with a plate and leave to steam.

03 Preheat your oven to 220°C/200°C fan/gas mark 7. Tip the hazelnuts onto a baking tray and toast in the oven for 4–5 minutes until just golden.

04 Meanwhile, trim the ends off the courgettes and slice lengthways into thin strips. Halve the Little Gem lettuces. Spread both out in a single layer across two roasting trays, laying the lettuce cut-side up. Drizzle over a good glug olive oil and season with salt and black pepper. Set aside.

05 Romesco time. Leave the toasted hazelnuts to cool slightly. Come back to the peppers, remove most of the skin and all the seeds – they should come off easily in your hands, be careful if they're still a little hot.

06 Peel the garlic and put in a food processor with the peppers, most of the hazelnuts, 1 tablespoon of sherry, 1 teaspoon of the smoked paprika and 4 tablespoons of olive oil. Blitz to a chunky paste. Season with salt and black pepper to taste, adding more vinegar if you like.

07 Put the courgettes and lettuces in the oven. Roast for 10–12 minutes while you fry the fish, until the lettuce is a little charred and the courgettes are tender.

08 Get a large non-stick frying pan over a super-high heat. Pat the cod dry, sprinkle over the remaining paprika and season with salt and black

pepper. Once the pan is searingly hot drizzle in some olive oil. Add the fish and fry for 2–3 minutes on each side until just cooked through.

09   Roughly chop the parsley and remaining hazelnuts. Cut the lemon into four wedges.

10   Spoon the romesco onto the side of four plates and lay the cod on top. Divide the roasted courgettes and Little Gem lettuce leaves between the plates. Drizzle over a splash more vinegar and olive oil. Scatter over the hazelnuts and parsley. Serve with the lemon wedges.

BURRATA WITH NDUJA DRESSING

GF · ⏱ 15 MINS · SERVES 4

Nothing goes better with a creamy ball of burrata than a fiery
nduja dressing. Not only is this starter visually stunning but it maintains
a perfect balance between the poles of salt, fat, acid and heat.
Samin Nosrat would be proud of this one.

GLUTEN-FREE: If serving with bread, choose a gluten-free alternative.

BUDGET HACK: If you can't find nduja, fry spicy chopped chorizo in olive oil and use as the dressing.

6 LARGE RIPE TOMATOES
A SPLASH OF RED WINE VINEGAR
50G (1¾OZ) BLANCHED ALMONDS
100G (3½OZ) NDUJA
1 SMALL BUNCH OF FRESH MINT
3 × 150G (5½OZ) BALLS OF BURRATA
OLIVE OIL
SALT AND BLACK PEPPER
BREAD OF YOUR CHOICE, TO SERVE
   → **WE LOVE THIS WITH OUR ROSEMARY AND OLIVE FOCACCIA (SEE PAGE 179)**

01   Slice the tomatoes into thin rounds. Lay, overlapping slightly, onto a large serving plate. Season well with salt and black pepper then drizzle over a good splash of red wine vinegar.

02   Toast the almonds in a dry frying pan over a medium heat until nice and golden. Tip out onto a chopping board.

03   Place the pan back over a low heat. Drizzle in a splash of olive oil and add the nduja. Allow to gently melt.

04   Roughly chop the toasted almonds and tear the mint leaves. Place the burratas on top of the tomatoes. Spoon over all the warm nduja oil and scatter over the almonds and mint.

05   Bring to the table for everyone to tuck in. Serve with your choice of bread for mopping.

ROSEMARY & OLIVE FOCACCIA

VG, DF · ⏱ 5 HRS 30 MINS + OVERNIGHT FERMENTING · MAKES 1 LOAF

The ultimate focaccia recipe, like the ciabatta, requires an
overnight starter called a biga. Think of it as bread supercharger (or
performance enhancer) as it's what makes the bread so light.
This is one of our favourite recipes.

FOR THE BIGA

180G (6½OZ) STRONG WHITE BREAD
   FLOUR
110ML (3¾OZ) WARM WATER
A LARGE PINCH OF DRIED INSTANT
   YEAST

FOR THE DOUGH

275G (9¾OZ) STRONG WHITE BREAD
   FLOUR
250ML (9FL OZ) WARM WATER
7 TBSP EXTRA-VIRGIN OLIVE OIL, PLUS
   EXTRA TO SERVE
1 TSP SALT
1¼ TSP DRIED INSTANT YEAST
4 FRESH ROSEMARY SPRIGS
A HANDFUL OF GREEN OLIVES
FLAKY SEA SALT

01   The night before you want to make your focaccia, make the overnight biga. Tip the flour, water and yeast into a bowl and mix really well until no lumps of flour remain. Cover with cling film with a small hole poked into it and leave for 12 hours.

02   The next day, make the dough. Tip the flour, warm water, 3 tablespoons of the oil, yeast, salt and overnight biga into a large bowl and using clean hands mix everything together until fully incorporated. It'll feel like a scarily wet dough MOB, but stick with it!

03   Leave for 30 minutes covered with the cling film, then wet your hands and pick up a corner of the dough, stretch it up without ripping it and fold it towards you, up and over the dough. Repeat with the other three corners, wetting your hands each time. You should feel the dough tighten up a little as you go. Repeat this every 30 minutes for another 1 hour, then leave the dough to prove for another 1 hour 30 minutes untouched (so 3 hours in total).

04   Oil the bottom and sides of a deep baking tray (roughly 20 × 30cm/ 8 × 12in) and tip in the dough. Use wet hands to gently pull and work the dough so that it roughly fills the tin. Leave for 2 hours, covered with a tea towel, until really puffy and bubbly.

05   Heat the oven to 220°C/200°C fan/gas mark 7.

06   Strip the rosemary into a small bowl. Add the remaining 4 tablespoons of oil. Spoon over the surface of the focaccia then wet your fingers and make dimples all over the bread. Dot with the olives, pushing these into the dough slightly. Sprinkle with flaky sea salt and put into the oven for 30–35 minutes or until really golden on top.

07   Carefully slide out onto a cooling rack, then drizzle with a little more oil to serve.

01 The night before you want to bake, make your biga.

02 Tip the flour, warm water, oil, salt and overnight biga into a large bowl.

05 Repeat this every 30 minutes for another 1 hour, then leave the dough to prove for another 1 hour 30 minutes.

06 Oil the bottom and sides of a deep baking tray and tip in the dough.

03 Mix together until fully incorporated.

04 Stretch and fold the dough until it starts to tighten.

07 Spoon the rosemary oil over the dough.

08 Wet your fingers and make dimples all over the bread.

LAMB NECK OSSO BUCO WITH CHOPPED SALSA VERDE

GF · ⏱ 3 HRS · SERVES 4

This is everything you want to eat: slow-braised saucy lamb, cheesy polenta, and a tangy, fresh salsa verde. We use bone-in lamb neck chops here instead of a classic veal shank. Much cheaper. Just as delicious.

GLUTEN-FREE: Check the label on your stock.

BUDGET HACK: Lamb neck is very inexpensive and when cooked right melts off the bone.

4 THICK BONE-IN LAMB NECK CHOPS →
   GET THESE FROM A BUTCHER. TELL
   THEM YOU WANT THE THICKNESS
   OF A VEAL SHANK IF ASKED

1 ONION

2 CARROTS

2 CELERY STICKS

5 GARLIC CLOVES

3 TBSP TOMATO PURÉE

A HANDFUL OF FRESH THYME

1 LARGE GLASS OF WHITE WINE
   (250ML/9FL OZ)

2 LITRES (3½ PINTS) CHICKEN STOCK

100G (3½OZ) PARMESAN CHEESE, PLUS
   THE RIND → CUT THE RIND OFF THE
   PARMESAN AND ADD TO THE SAUCE
   FOR MAX FLAVOUR

1 BUNCH OF FRESH PARSLEY

2 TBSP CAPERS

1–2 TBSP RED WINE VINEGAR

200G (7OZ) QUICK-COOK POLENTA
   (SOMETIMES CALLED PRE-COOKED)

50G (1¾OZ) BUTTER

OLIVE OIL

SALT AND BLACK PEPPER

01   Get a large saucepan or casserole over a high heat. Season the lamb neck chops generously with salt and black pepper. Drizzle some olive oil into the pan. Fry the meat for around 5 minutes until evenly browned. Transfer to a plate.

02   Meanwhile, peel and chop the onion, then chop the carrots and celery. Once the browned meat is on a plate, scrape the veg into the pan. Turn down the heat and cook, stirring occasionally, until soft.

03   Peel and finely chop four of the garlic cloves. Add them to the pan, cook for 1 minute more then stir in the tomato purée and thyme. Pour in the white wine. Once mostly bubbled away, put the lamb back into the pan, pour in 1 litre (1¾ pints) of chicken stock and add the rind from the Parmesan. Bring to a boil then reduce the heat to low, season with salt and black pepper, put on a lid and simmer away for 2–2½ hours until the lamb is completely tender. The meat will come away from the bone.

04   Carefully transfer the lamb onto a plate. Turn up the heat and reduce the sauce then return the meat to the pan and keep warm. Season to taste with salt and black pepper.

05   Salsa verde time. Grate the remaining garlic clove into a small bowl. Finely chop the parsley and roughly chop the capers. Scrape into the bowl. Add 1 tablespoon of red wine vinegar and 3 tablespoons of olive oil. Season to taste with salt and black pepper and add more vinegar if you like the sharpness.

06   Pour the remaining chicken stock into a large saucepan and bring to the boil. Finely grate the Parmesan cheese onto a chopping board.

07   Grab a whisk. Pour the polenta into the boiling stock, whisking continuously to combine. Keep whisking for a minute or so to get out any

lumps as the polenta cooks and thickens. Once it is at the consistency of a loose mash, take off the heat, stir in the butter and Parmesan and let it melt. Season to taste with salt and black pepper.

08 Spoon the polenta into four bowls. Top each one with the lamb neck osso bucco then spoon over the salsa verde to serve.

HERBY RICOTTA GNOCCHI

V · ⏱ 45 MINS · SERVES 4

This gnocchi recipe calls for ricotta instead of potato in its dough. The
result? The lightest, most delicate pillows of pasta you could ask for.
Served in a brown butter sauce with capers and toasted pumpkin seeds,
this dish is super-light yet still feels indulgently rich.

BUDGET HACK: Use one type of
herb rather than a mixed bunch.

2 × 250G (9OZ) POTS OF RICOTTA

3 TBSP PUMPKIN SEEDS

1 LARGE BUNCH OF FRESH MIXED
    HERBS (WE LIKE PARSLEY AND DILL)

80G (2¾OZ) '00' FLOUR, PLUS EXTRA
    FOR DUSTING

2 EGG YOLKS → FREEZE THE WHITES
    FOR ANOTHER TIME

1 LEMON

50G (1¾OZ) PECORINO CHEESE, PLUS
    EXTRA TO SERVE

120G (4¼OZ) BUTTER

2 TBSP CAPERS

SALT AND BLACK PEPPER

01   Drain the ricotta in a sieve to get rid of any excess water then tip
into a large bowl. Toast the pumpkin seeds in a dry frying pan until they
begin to pop. Set aside.

02   Gnocchi time. Finely chop most of the herbs (stalks and all). Add
the flour, egg yolks and herbs to the ricotta. Finely grate in the lemon
zest and the Pecorino cheese. Season generously with salt and black
pepper then mix everything together to form a dough.

03   Bring a large saucepan of salted water to the boil.

04   Tip the gnocchi dough onto a really well-floured surface. With
floured hands knead briefly until smooth – the dough should feel light
and a little sticky to touch but keep its shape well.

05   Cut the dough into six, then flouring your hands roll one piece into
a sausage around 2cm (¾in) thick. Cut into bite-sized pieces. Transfer to
a large well-floured baking tray. Repeat with the remaining dough.

06   Working in batches, drop the gnocchi into the boiling water. Cook
for 1–2 minutes until they float. With a slotted spoon, transfer to a clean
baking tray. Repeat until all the gnocchi has been cooked.

07   Get a large frying pan over a medium heat. Add the butter and
let it melt until it turns lightly brown and begins to smell nutty. Add
in the toasted pumpkin seeds, capers and gnocchi. Give everything a
good toss to warm the gnocchi back through. Cut the lemon in half and
squeeze in some of the juice. Season to taste with salt and black pepper.

08   Divide the gnocchi and brown butter sauce between four bowls.
Grate over some Pecorino cheese and tear over the remaining herbs
to serve.

WHOLE-BAKED SEABASS WITH GINGER, LEMONGRASS, CHILLI & COCONUT RICE

DF, GF · ⏱ 55 MINS · SERVES 4

Cooking a whole fish in a foil parcel ensures you get the
flakiest, most succulent fish possible. Here, it's steamed with
ginger, lime, and lemongrass to give the dish a much-needed lift.
Served with creamy coconut rice, and loads of toppings,
this is a recipe you'll keep coming back to.

GLUTEN-FREE: If you're cooking gluten-free, substitute the soy sauce for tamari.

BUDGET HACK: Replace the crispy onions with some finely sliced spring onion on top.

THUMB-SIZED PIECE OF FRESH GINGER
3 SPRING ONIONS
2 LEMONGRASS STALKS
2 LIMES
A SPLASH OF SESAME OIL
2 MEDIUM WHOLE SEABASS → GET THE
   FISHMONGER TO SCALE AND GUT
   THEM FOR YOU
300G (10½OZ) JASMINE RICE
400ML (14FL OZ) TIN OF COCONUT MIK
A SMALL HANDFUL OF FRESH
   CORIANDER
3 TBSP CRISPY ONION
SALT AND BLACK PEPPER
SOY SAUCE, TO SERVE
CHILLI OIL WITH SEDIMENT (WE USED
   LEE KUM KEE), TO SERVE

YOU WILL ALSO NEED FOIL.

01   Preheat your oven to 200°C/180°C fan/gas mark 6.

02   Leaving the skin on the ginger, thinly slice. Thinly slice the spring onions and one lemongrass stalk. Slice one lime into rounds.

03   Line your largest baking tray with two big pieces of foil (the foil needs to be large enough to encase the fish). Drizzle over a little sesame oil – this will stop the fish from sticking.

04   Make three diagonal cuts into the flesh of both seabass, on each side. Season both fish inside and out with salt and black pepper, then stuff with the ginger, spring onions, lemongrass and lime slices. Lay them next to each other in the centre of the foil and drizzle over a little sesame oil. Bring up the sides of the foil, scrunch together at the top to create a loose-tented parcel. Roast in the oven for 35–45 minutes, depending on the size of the fish, until the meat is coming away from the bone.

05   Meanwhile, make the coconut rice. Measure the rice into a bowl. Fill with cold water and use your fingertips to rub the grains of rice together – this helps get rid of excess starch. Once the water has turned milky, drain and repeat.

06   Tip the drained rice into a medium-sized saucepan and pour in the coconut milk. Half fill the tin with water then add this too. Season with a good pinch of salt and chuck in the remaining lemongrass stick. Get your pan over a high heat and bring to the boil then lower the heat and cover. Simmer away for 10–15 minutes until all the liquid has evaporated. Turn off the heat and keep the coconut rice warm with the lid on.

07 Cut the lime into four wedges. Roughly chop the coriander (stalks and all).

08 Once the seabass is cooked, remove from the oven. Scatter the coriander, crispy onions and lime wedges over the cooked seabass. Serve out of the tray alongside the rice, with some soy sauce and chilli oil for people to help themselves.

6

AROUND THE WORLD

The most comforting dishes
from different contributors from
cuisines across the globe.

BAJA TACOS

○ 50 MINS · SERVES 4 · BY BREDDOS TACOS

Nud is the founder of Breddos (arguably the best tacos in London).
These are his fish tacos and the way he preps the fish should be
followed to the letter. Don't worry about the lumps in the batter, it'll
make it extra crispy! You will need a cooking thermometer for this.

100G (3½OZ) PLAIN FLOUR

250G (9OZ) BONELESS SKINLESS COD
FILLET

500ML (17FL OZ) RAPESEED OIL

FOR THE SALSA

1 MANGO

1 JALAPEÑO CHILLI

1 BUNCH OF FRESH MINT

1 LIME

A PINCH OF SUGAR

OLIVE OIL

SALT AND BLACK PEPPER

FOR THE CHIPOTLE MAYONNAISE

100ML (3½FL OZ) MAYONNAISE

2 TBSP SRIRACHA

2 TBSP CHIPOTLE IN ADOBO

FOR THE WET FISH BATTER

150G (5½OZ) PLAIN FLOUR

½ TSP BAKING POWDER

1 TSP FINE SALT

100ML (3½FL OZ) LIGHT BEER OR COLD
SPARKLING WATER

100ML (3½FL OZ) VODKA

TO SERVE

½ RED CABBAGE

8 SMALL CORN TORTILLAS

2 LIMES

1 BUNCH OF FRESH CORIANDER

01   Start by making your mango salsa. Dice your mango into small chunks, finely chop your jalapeños and mint then mix together in a bowl. Cut the lime in half. Squeeze in the lime juice and add a pinch of salt, black pepper, sugar and a drizzle of olive oil. Set aside.

02   Now for the chipotle mayo, it's super-easy! Just mix together your mayo, Sriracha, and chipotle then set aside.

03   Quarter your cabbage and slice it into thin strips. Set aside.

04   On to the wet fish batter. Into a bowl, add 150g (5½oz) of plain flour, baking powder, salt, a crack of black pepper, beer or sparkling water and vodka. Whisk well to create a smooth batter.

05   Frying time. Add the remaining flour (100g/3½oz) to a bowl. Chop your fish into eight strips and dip each chunk into the flour, shake off any excess then dip it straight into the wet fish batter, making sure it is thoroughly coated.

06   Heat your rapeseed oil to 180°C/350°F in a large frying pan. Then, carefully lower the fish into the oil and repeat for all fish chunks. Leave to fry for about 5 minutes until golden and crunchy.

07   Once your fish is ready, place it on some kitchen roll to cool down. Meanwhile, warm up your tortillas by placing them in a dry frying pan over a low heat until slightly browned.

08   Time to assemble! Cut the limes in half. Take a tortilla, place some red cabbage on the bottom, followed by your chipotle mayonnaise, then the fried fish and a teaspoon of the mango salsa. Top with a couple of coriander leaves, a squeeze of lime juice and a pinch of salt. Tuck in and enjoy!

SPELT VARENYKY WITH KRAUT, CHESTNUTS & CARAMELIZED ONIONS

V · ⏱ 1 HR 45 MINUTES PLUS OVERNIGHT SOAKING · SERVES 2 (MAKES 16) · BY OLIA HERCULES

Using spelt to make the dough is more nutritious and adds more flavour.
Variations of this filling are used in northwestern parts of Ukraine.
These are very good tossed in Asian-style crispy chilli and garlic oil.

FOR THE FILLING

2 TBSP NEUTRAL OIL, SUCH AS RAPESEED OR GROUNDNUT
1 MEDIUM ONION, FINELY DICED
1 SMALL CARROT, ROUGHLY GRATED
100G (3½OZ) SAUERKRAUT, DRAINED
100G (3½OZ) MUSHROOMS, FINELY CHOPPED OR ROUGHLY GRATED ON A BOX GRATER (IF USING BUTTON MUSHROOMS)
100G (3½OZ) COOKED CHESTNUTS, FINELY CHOPPED (OPTIONAL)
SEA SALT AND BLACK PEPPER

FOR THE DOUGH

110ML (3¾FL OZ) WATER
210G (7½OZ) SPELT FLOUR
PLAIN FLOUR OR SEMOLINA AND POLENTA, TO PREVENT STICKING
50G (1¾OZ) BUTTER, MELTED

YOGHURT OR CRÈME FRAÎCHE, TO SERVE
PICKLED JALAPEÑOS AND/OR FERMENTED CHILLI SAUCE, TO SERVE

YOU WILL ALSO NEED A ROLLING PIN.

01   Heat 1 tablespoon of the oil in a large frying pan and add the onion. Cook them over a medium–low heat (I sometimes cover with a wet cartouche to speed things along) until the onion is translucent.

02   Add the grated carrot and cook until the onion and carrot start turning golden. Add a splash of water or vegetable stock and scrape at the pan if needed. Then add the kraut and a little more oil if the pan is too dry and cook for another 5–10 minutes. Then scrape the onion, carrot and kraut into a bowl.

03   Add more oil to the same pan and cook the chopped mushrooms over a medium–high heat, stirring from time to time, until nicely browned. Add this, with the chestnuts, to the onion mix, season well with sea salt and black pepper and let the filling cool.

04   Prepare a flat tray lightly floured or sprinkled with semolina and polenta, and set a large pot of salted water on to boil. Have a large bowl ready with some melted butter. My grandmother called the melted butter 'krynychka' – a well – just to explain how much she actually put! You can put as much as you like.

05   Now for the dough, once it is made it loses its binding powers very quickly, so I actually do it in two batches. I put half of the the cold water into a medium bowl and mix in half of the flour, then knead it briefly to combine on a floured table. Now, roll the dough into a sausage shape and cut eight 20g (¾oz) pieces with a knife or a dough scraper. Flatten each piece with the palm of your hand and then roll them out into a circle, as thin as you can manage. Now put a tablespoon (16–18g/½–¾oz) of the filling in the centre of each circle and close the edges to make a half-moon. Now you can leave them as they are or crimp the edges.

06 Put the varenyky on your prepped tray as you go along and cover with a towel so they don't dry out. Repeat the process until you have your 16 dumplings.

07 Gently drop them one by one into the boiling water, give them a stir with a large spoon to make sure none of them are stuck to the bottom. Boil for about 6–8 minutes, they will float to the top when ready.

08 Drain and pop the varenyky into the bowl of butter and toss them in it. Serve with yoghurt or crème fraîche and some pickles like shop-bought jalapeños, homemade fermented chillies or a fermented chilli sauce.

KING PRAWN NYONYA CURRY LAKSA

GF, DF · ⏱ 1 HR 10 MINS · SERVES 6 · BY MANDY YIN, SAMBAL SHIOK LAKSA BAR

This is my signature curry laksa, with a strong chilli and shrimp kick. In Malaysia, we tend to save cooking laksa at home for special occasions due to its time-consuming method and lengthy ingredient list. It is a perfect weekend project. The majority of the preparation can be done a day or two in advance and the broth develops in flavour if left overnight.

GLUTEN-FREE: If cooking gluten-free, check the labels of the stocks and Worcestershire sauce or brown sauce, if using.

FOR THE SPICE PASTE
150G (5FL OZ) VEGETABLE OIL
1 MEDIUM ONION (APPROX. 300G/10½OZ), ROUGHLY CHOPPED
7½CM (3IN) PIECE OF FRESH GINGER, PEELED AND ROUGHLY CHOPPED
8 GARLIC CLOVES, PEELED
3 FRESH RED CHILLIES, STALKS REMOVED THEN ROUGHLY CHOPPED
15 DRIED CHILLIES, SOAKED IN HOT WATER FOR 30 MINUTES, DRAINED
1½ TBSP GROUND CUMIN
1½ TBSP GROUND TURMERIC
3 TBSP GROUND CORIANDER
3 TBSP CHILLI POWDER
50G (1¾OZ) SHRIMP PASTE (THE MALAYSIAN/INDONESIAN BLOCKS OF SHRIMP PASTE OTHERWIE THAI GAPI SHRIMP PASTE)

01   Blend all of the spice paste ingredients in a food processor until it achieves the consistency of a smooth fine paste. Place a large non-stick frying pan over a low–medium heat and add the spice paste. Cook, continuously stirring, for 15–20 minutes until it is a rich dark red brown colour and the oil separates from the paste. Ideally leave for at least 24 hours in the fridge for the fried paste to develop maximum flavour before using it to make the broth.

02   Fill a large saucepan with water and bring to the boil.

03   Add the laksa broth ingredients to another large saucepan with the fried spice paste. Bring to the boil then simmer gently for 20 minutes. Turn off the heat, then remove the lemongrass and season with sugar and salt to taste.

04   Whilst the laksa broth is simmering, deal with the noodles and toppings. Steep the rice vermicelli in water that has just boiled for 10 minutes, then drain in a sieve. Blanch the following in water at a rolling boil one after the other: beansprouts for 10 seconds, green beans for 3 minutes and prawns for 90 seconds. Use a slotted spoon to remove each ingredient from the boiling water. Refresh each ingredient in a colander under cold running water immediately after removing from the boiling water to stop them cooking in residual heat. Drain well.

05   Portion the noodles, beansprouts, green beans and prawns into six bowls ready for serving. Pour the hot laksa broth into each of the bowls and enjoy immediately!

FOR THE LAKSA BROTH

1⅓ LITRES (2½ PINTS) GOOD-QUALITY
    CHICKEN STOCK

2 × 400G (14OZ) TINS OF COCONUT
    MILK

90G (3¼OZ) DARK BROWN SUGAR

3 TBSP TAMARIND PASTE
    (OR SUBSTITUTE WITH
    WORCESTERSHIRE SAUCE OR
    BROWN SAUCE)

2 LEMONGRASS STEMS, POUNDED
    WITH A PESTLE TO RELEASE JUICES

SALT AND SOFT BROWN SUGAR, TO
    TASTE

TOPPINGS

400G (14 OZ) RICE VERMICELLI

120G (4¼OZ) BEANSPROUTS

120G (4¼OZ) GREEN BEANS, CUT INTO
    5CM (2IN) LENGTHS

36 RAW PEELED DEVEINED KING
    PRAWNS (SIX PRAWNS PER PERSON)

YOU WILL ALSO NEED A FOOD
PROCESSOR.

DAL MAKHANI

V, GF · ⏱ 2 HRS + OVERNIGHT SOAKING · SERVES 4 · BY SONALI SHAH

I count myself really lucky to have grown up around amazing cooks like
my mum and nani (her mum). Whilst we ate all kinds of exciting foods, if I had
to pick an ultimate comfort meal, my mum's urad dal always stands out.
A good dal doesn't need fancy garnishes, serve it up with some fluffy rice or
bread and get stuck in. This recipe freezes surprisingly well (I used to
take bags of it to uni!) and can easily be made vegan.

GLUTEN-FREE: Check the label
on your garam masala if cooking
gluten-free.

MAKE IT VEGAN: Use vegetable
oil instead of ghee, dairy-free
butter and dairy-free cream.

200G (7OZ) BLACK URAD DAL

1 TSP CUMIN SEEDS

2 MEDIUM ONIONS, PEELED

20G GINGER, PEELED

5–6 GARLIC CLOVES

4 TBSP GHEE (OR VEGETABLE OIL)

½ × 400G TIN OF CHOPPED TOMATOES

1 TBSP TOMATO PASTE

1 TSP GROUND TURMERIC

1–2 TSP CHILLI POWDER (DEPENDING
     ON HOW SPICY YOU LIKE IT)

1 TBSP GROUND CORIANDER

½ TSP GARAM MASALA

1 TSP METHI (DRIED FENUGREEK)

80G (2¾OZ) UNSALTED BUTTER (OR
     DAIRY-FREE BUTTER), PLUS EXTRA
     TO SERVE (OPTIONAL)

3–4 TBSP DOUBLE CREAM (OR DAIRY-
     FREE CREAM)

HANDFUL OF FRESH CORIANDER,
     CHOPPED

RICE, PARATHA OR CHAPATI, TO SERVE

01   Add the urad dal to a bowl, cover with hot water and leave to soak
overnight.

02   The next day add 2 litres (3½ pints) of water to a large saucepan and
bring to the boil. Meanwhile, drain the urad dal. Once the water is boiling,
add the drained urad dal and simmer for 1 hour–1 hour 30 minutes or
until the lentil grains are soft and creamy when pressed between your
fingers (this step can be done ahead of time).

03   Whilst the dal is cooking, add the onions to a food processor and
blitz until a paste forms. Remove to a bowl, then blitz the ginger and
garlic in the same way.

04   Heat the ghee in a separate saucepan over a medium heat. Once
hot, add the cumin seeds and when they start to sizzle add the onion
paste with a generous pinch of salt.

05   Once the onions have softened, add the chopped tomatoes,
tomato paste, ginger and garlic paste, turmeric, chilli powder, ground
coriander, garam masala and methi. Bring to a simmer then cook for
5–10 minutes or until the oil begins to separate – this mixture is known
as your 'vaghar' (or tempering mix).

06   When the dal is cooked, carefully pour the vaghar into the dal and
stir well. Add in the butter and cook for a further 8–10 minutes or until
combined. Add more water at this stage to loosen if required.

07   Once the dal has come together, stir most of the double cream in.

08   Serve drizzled with the reserved double cream, chopped coriander
and a knob of butter if you like.

CHEAT'S CHICKEN BIRYANI

GF · ⏱ 2 HRS · SERVES 4 · BY MALLIKA BASU

FOR THE CHICKEN

1KG (2LB 4OZ) SKIN-ON, BONE-IN
    CHICKEN THIGHS AND DRUMSTICKS
2 TBSP GREEK-NATURAL YOGHURT
2 MEDIUM ONIONS
2½CM (1IN) PIECE OF FRESH GINGER
4 GARLIC CLOVES
4 TBSP NEUTRAL OIL SUCH AS
    VEGETABLE OR SUNFLOWER
3 TBSP BIRYANI SPICE BLEND
½ TSP SALT

FOR THE RICE

500G (1LB 2OZ) EXTRA- LONG GRAIN
    BASMATI RICE (I LIKE TILDA)
2 BLACK CARDAMOM PODS
4 GREEN CARDAMOM PODS
5CM (2IN) CINNAMON STICK
4 CLOVES
2½ TSP SALT

TO GARNISH

3 TBSP WHOLE MILK
3 PINCHES OF SAFFRON
1 LARGE ONION
1½ TBSP NEUTRAL OIL SUCH AS
    VEGETABLE, SUNFLOWER OR
    GROUNDNUT OIL
A PINCH OF SALT
A PINCH OF CASTER SUGAR
1 TBSP GHEE OR BUTTER
½ NUTMEG
2 TSP ROSE WATER
MIXED RAITA, TO SERVE (OPTIONAL)

YOU WILL ALSO NEED FOIL.

A fragrant feast of regal proportions from the courts of India's Mughal emperors. This cheat's version uses ready-made Biryani spice mix and takes a lot less time to cook than the four hours-plus it normally should. Buy the very best quality extra-long grain basmati rice you can, punchy saffron and whole nutmeg. Ghee is Indian clarified butter, though butter will do.

01 For the garnish, warm the milk in a bowl or cup and drop the saffron in to infuse.

02 Skin the chicken and toss it in the yoghurt. Peel the onions, garlic and ginger. Thinly slice the onions and finely grate the ginger and garlic. Heat the oil in a large saucepan over a high heat. When it's hot, toss in the sliced onions and sauté for five minutes until they take on colour.

03 Now, add in the ginger and garlic and cook them for 5 minutes, stirring regularly. Mix in the chicken and biryani spice blend. Stir everything together thoroughly for 5 minutes to seal the chicken.

04 Pour in 250ml (9fl oz) hot water, add the salt then cook uncovered over a medium–high heat for 30 minutes. You need to keep an eye on the curry, stirring it regularly to make sure it doesn't get stuck to the pan or burn. Add 125ml (4fl oz) more water if either of these threaten to happen. When the curry is thick and clings to the chicken, turn the heat off and leave it to sit.

05 Meanwhile, onto the rice. Place the basmati in a sieve and wash it thoroughly under the cold tap until the water draining is clear. Place the whole spices into a large saucepan and tip in the washed rice and salt. Pour in 1.2 litres (2 pints) hot water. Bring to the boil and then lower to a high simmer. Cover and cook for 10 minutes. Drain in a sieve as soon as it's cooked.

06 Back to the garnish. Peel and finely slice the large onion. Get a medium frying pan over a medium–high heat and drizzle in the oil. Add the onion with the salt and sugar and fry until caramelized. Turn the heat off and leave to sit.

07 Time to assemble the biryani with its characteristic layering. First, preheat the oven to 180°C/160°C fan/gas mark 4. Now rub ½ tablespoon of the ghee or butter onto the base of a casserole or ovenproof deep pan/dish big enough to snugly accommodate the ingredients with a tight-fitting lid.

08 Spread half the rice evenly on top of this, removing and keeping safe any whole spices you come across. Grate a quarter of the nutmeg on top and dot over half of the milk and saffron mixture. Now place the meat along with its curry on top of the rice evenly in a single layer. You can leave the oil behind in the pan if you prefer.

09 Then spread the remaining rice on top, placing the whole spices back on. Dot the remaining ghee on top with the rose water and the remaining milky saffron then grate over the remaining nutmeg. Spread the caramelized onion all over. Seal the top with foil and then stick the lid on.

10 Place the pot in the centre of the oven and cook for 20 minutes. When it's done, bring it to the table and unveil it in its full glory. If you've cooked this the day before, leave it to cool in the pot and refrigerate it until you're ready to eat.

11 This needs little else to go with it, but you could serve it with a mixed raita of chopped cucumber, tomatoes and onions tossed in yoghurt and topped with chilli powder.

JOK MU

GF, DF · ⏱ 1 HR 10 MINS + 2 HRS SOAKING · SERVES 4 · BY JOHN CHANTARASAK, ANGLOTHAI

Jok is a hugely popular comfort food in Thailand that is eaten to cure hangovers and sickness. Although the name 'rice porridge' can sound dull to westerners, the dish is full of flavour and is incredibly moreish.

GLUTEN-FREE: If you're cooking gluten-free, substitute the soy sauce for tamari.

FOR THE PORK BALLS
HANDFUL CORIANDER STEMS OR ROOT
3 FAT GARLIC CLOVES, CHOPPED
1 TSP SALT
½ TSP WHITE PEPPERCORNS
1 TBSP LIGHT SOY SAUCE
1 TSP OYSTER SAUCE
160G (5¾OZ) FATTY PORK MINCE
1½ LITRES (2½ PINTS) LIGHT PORK
    STOCK OR WATER

FOR THE JOK MU
250G (9OZ) BROKEN RICE (OR
    JASMINE RICE PULSED IN A FOOD
    PROCESSOR), RINSED AND SOAKED
    IN COLD WATER FOR 2 HOURS
1¼ LITRES (2 PINTS) PORK BALL
    POACHING LIQUOR (SEE ABOVE)
1 PANDAN LEAF, KNOTTED (OPTIONAL)
4 TBSP LIGHT SOY SAUCE, TO TASTE
1 TSP OYSTER SAUCE
1 TSP CASTER OR GRANULATED SUGAR
LARGE KNOB OF FRESH GINGER,
    THINLY SHREDDED
4 TBSP SPRING ONION GREEN TOPS,
    THINLY SLICED
2 MEDIUM EGGS
A HANDFUL OF FRESH CORIANDER,
    ROUGHLY CHOPPED
CRACKED WHITE PEPPER

01 Start by making the pork balls. Using a pestle and mortar, pound the coriander, garlic, salt and white peppercorns into a smooth paste. Add the light soy sauce and oyster sauce then combine with the pork mince. Mix until well combined.

02 Bring the pork stock or water to boil, then reduce to a simmer. Pinch the pork mixture into rustic balls (around 2cm/¾in) and simmer in the stock until cooked through, around 10–12 minutes. They should become firm and slightly bouncy. Remove with a slotted spoon and set aside.

03 Bring the pork stock back to the boil. Drain the broken rice and add to the boiling pork stock, along with the pandanas leaf, if using, stirring the rice well to help it break up and prevent any sticking on the base of the pan.

04 Reduce to the lowest possible heat, cover with a lid and simmer very gently for 35–40 minutes, stirring periodically, until the rice resembles a porridge texture. You may need to add additional stock or water during the cooking process to achieve your desired thickness.

05 Season with the light soy sauce, oyster sauce and sugar, taste and adjust the seasoning to your liking.

06 Add the pork balls to the rice with the ginger and spring onions. Crack the eggs into the rice and leave to simmer very gently for a minute to slightly set the eggs. Stir the rice once or twice to fold the eggs through the rice.

07 Serve sprinkled with the coriander and plenty of cracked white pepper.

CHICKEN PHO – PHỞ GÀ

GF, DF · ⏱ 2 HRS 15 MINS · SERVES 4 · BY CHEF THUY DIEM PHAM, THE LITTLE VIET KITCHEN

This dish never fails to impress. The love starts from the moment you first gather the ingredients and start to slowly layer the rich flavours together; and finishes many hours later with the joy on the faces of your diners. Chicken pho is as close as you can get to giving someone a hug, through food. It truly showcases Vietnamese flavours and culinary techniques and I am so happy to share my recipe with you here.

GLUTEN-FREE: Check the label of your hoisin sauce if cooking gluten-free and find an alternative if necessary.

400G (14OZ) DRIED PHO NOODLES

200G (7OZ) BEANSPROUTS

2 SPRING ONIONS (WHITE AND GREEN PARTS), FINELY CHOPPED

2 RED CHILLIES, SLICED

8 SPRIGS OF FRESH THAI BASIL

12 SPRIGS OF FRESH CORIANDER

4 TSP CRISPY FRIED SHALLOTS OR ONIONS

1 LIME, QUARTERED

4 TSP HOISIN SAUCE, TO SERVE

4 TSP SRIRACHA, TO SERVE

FOR THE BROTH

4 ONIONS

50G (1¾OZ) FRESH GINGER

12 STAR ANISE

2 TSP CORIANDER SEEDS

1 LARGE CHICKEN (APPROX. 1.75KG/4LB)

1 MEDIUM DAIKON, OR 1 WHOLE SWEDE IF YOU CAN'T FIND

4 TBSP FISH SAUCE

90G (3¼OZ) ROCK SUGAR, CRUSHED, OR GRANULATED SUGAR

1 TSP SALT

01   Start with the broth. Roast the onions and ginger (keep the peels on) for approximately 5 minutes directly over an open flame, until you see the juice of the onion bubbling on the surface and the ginger is fully blackened. Wash under cold water and rub the blackened outer layers away. Alternatively, if you don't have a gas stove, roast at 190°C/170°C/ gas mark 5 for 20 minutes, peeling away the top layer when finished.

02   In a dry pan, roast the star anise and coriander seeds over a medium heat for 2–3 minutes. Peel and quarter the daikon.

03   Bring 4 litres (7 pints) of water to the boil in your largest stockpot/ saucepan and add the whole chicken, daikon, the roasted onions and ginger. Place the roasted spices into a spice strainer or muslin parcel and position it carefully at the bottom of the pot.

04   Lower the heat and simmer for 40–50 minutes, skimming away any foam that comes to the surface, until the chicken is cooked through. Do not stir the broth at all as this will make it cloudy.

05   Remove the chicken and place to one side to cool. Strain the broth, discarding the spices and any solids, and return to the pot. Add the fish sauce, sugar and salt to the broth and simmer for 20 minutes.

06   Meanwhile, soak the noodles in lukewarm water for 20 minutes. While the noodles are soaking, shred the chicken into large chunks. Drain the noodles. Bring a pan of water to the boil and cook the noodles very briefly for just 3 seconds. Drain well and leave to cool.

07   Take a quarter of the beansprouts and place into a bowl, then add a quarter of the noodles. Place the chicken on top. Now ladle the broth into the bowl leaving some room for adding the herbs. Sprinkle over the

spring onions, a couple of slices of chilli, the basil leaves, coriander and the crispy fried shallots. Repeat with the remaining three bowls.

08   Lastly, gently squeeze a lime quarter into each bowl to balance the flavours of the broth. This does have a large effect on the flavour so do be careful and make sure to add the right amount for your taste buds. Serve with hoisin sauce and Sriracha alongside for dipping.

PORK DUMPLINGS

DF · ⏱ 1 HR 20 MINS · SERVES 3–4 (MAKES ABOUT 32 DUMPLINGS) · BY CHUBBY DUMPLING

Pork dumplings are a classic! They should be bursting with flavour, soft, juicy and squidgy on the inside, with a crispy bottom. The recipe is easy to adjust, so can use whatever you have kicking about in your fridge.

FOR THE DOUGH

400G (14OZ) PLAIN FLOUR

170ML (5½FL OZ) WARM WATER

FOR THE FILLING

100G (3½OZ) PORK MINCE

40G (1½OZ) CHINESE CABBAGE, FINELY SHREDDED

20G (¾OZ) CHIVES, FINELY CHOPPED

40G (1½OZ) ONION, FINELY CHOPPED

SMALL PIECE OF FRESH GINGER, GRATED

A LARGE PINCH OF WHITE PEPPER

½ TSP SALT

1 FAT CLOVE GARLIC, GRATED

1 TSP CASTER SUGAR

2 TSP LIGHT SOY SAUCE

1 TBSP VEGETABLE OIL

½ TSP SESAME OIL

FOR THE DIPPING SAUCE

2 RED CHILLIES

3 TBSP LIGHT SOY SAUCE

YOU WILL ALSO NEED A PASTA MACHINE AND/OR A ROLLING PIN.

01   Mix the dough ingredients together in a large bowl then knead for about 5 minutes on a clean surface until a smooth, firm but pliable dough. Place back in the bowl, cover with cling film and leave the dough to rest for a while.

02   Meanwhile, make the filling. Mix the pork mince, cabbage and chives together in a bowl then weigh in all the other ingredients. Mix and set aside.

03   Knead the dough again then flatten slightly with a rolling pin. Cut into quarters, then feed one quarter through a pasta machine roller a few times down to the fourth thickest setting to get a consistent thickness to the sheet. Keep the rest of the dough covered until needed.

04   Using a circular cutter (about 7–8cm/2¾–3¼in in diameter), cut out circles in the dough to create your dumpling wrappers. Fill the dumplings with a teaspoon of filling, fold the dough in half and pinch together with your fingers. Pleat around the edge with your fingers to seal well – we find using a little water on your fingertips around the edge helps to seal them. Repeat with the remaining dough and filling. Transfer to a large baking tray.

05   Using a steamer or a steamer basket, steam the dumplings for 10 minutes. Get a large frying pan over a high heat and drizzle in a splash of veg oil. Add the dumplings and fry for 2 minutes. Alternatively bring a large saucepan of water to boil, then turn it down to a simmer. Gently place the dumplings in and move them about carefully so they don't stick to the bottom. Simmer for 5–6 minutes – make sure the water isn't boiling vigorously because otherwise the dumplings can break. Then fry for 2 minutes.

06   Meanwhile, make the dipping sauce. Finely chop the red chillies. Heat the veg oil in a small frying pan over a medium heat. Add the chillies and sauté until softened (don't let them burn). Pour the chillies and oil into a bowl and add the soy sauce (you can add more if you don't want it too spicy). Mix together and serve with the dumplings.

IF YOU DON'T HAVE A PASTA MAKER YOU CAN ROLL THE DUMPLINGS AS FOLLOWS:

· On a lightly floured surface, roll the dough into a long sausage that's about 2cm (¾in) in diameter.

· Using a knife, cut each length of dough into 2cm (¾in)-thick pieces. Each piece should weigh about 10–12g (¼–½oz).

· Roll each piece of dough into a small ball and then flatten it between your palms to create a disc.

· Place the disc on your floured surface and position your rolling pin between you and the base of the disc (the side closest to you). Roll the pin forward across the dough and back. You do not need to lift the rolling pin. Turn the dough 90 degrees and repeat. Turn the dough 90 degrees again and repeat one last time. This forms a circle and keeps the outer edges of the wrapper thinner so you can fold them together later.

RENDANG DAGING

DF, GF · ⏱ 3 HRS 30 MINS · SERVES 4 · BY LARA LEE

There are many interpretations of rendang, but the traditional is a slow-cooked dry beef curry that starts in a bath of white coconut milk and finishes a near-black colour when the oil splits from the milk and caramelizes the beef. The result is beef that is crispy on the outside and melt-in-the-mouth tender on the inside, laden with tropical spices and creamy, caramelized coconut. This recipe is my nod to wonderful traditional cooks. Serve with a heap of turmeric yellow rice, Padang green chilli sambal and a side of Asian greens.

1KG (2LB 4OZ) BRAISING BEEF, (SHIN OR BRISKET, TRIMMED OF FAT)

800ML (28FL OZ) COCONUT MILK

1 TSP SEA SALT

2 LEMONGRASS STALKS, BRUISED AND TIED IN A KNOT

3 BAY LEAVES

5 KAFFIR LIME LEAVES (OPTIONAL)

FOR THE SPICE PASTE

7 LONG RED CHILLIES, SLICED (DESEEDED IF YOU PREFER LESS HEAT)

3 SMALL BANANA SHALLOTS OR 6 THAI SHALLOTS, PEELED AND SLICED

5 GARLIC CLOVES, PEELED AND SLICED

8CM (3¼IN) FRESH GINGER (APPROX. 40G/1½OZ), PEELED AND SLICED

8CM (3¼IN) FRESH GALANGAL (ABOUT 40G/1½OZ), WOODY STEM REMOVED, THINLY SLICED (OPTIONAL)

3CM (1¼IN) FRESH TURMERIC (ABOUT 15G/½OZ), PEELED AND SLICED (OR 1 TSP GROUND TURMERIC)

2 TSP GROUND CORIANDER

1 TSP GROUND CUMIN

01　Place the spice paste ingredients in a small food processor and blend to a smooth paste. If the texture is too coarse, add a splash of the measured coconut milk and blend again.

02　Cut the beef into 3–4cm (1¼–1½in) chunks, removing any excess fat. Do not cut the chunks too small or the beef will disintegrate during the cooking process. Place the spice paste in a deep, heavy-based saucepan along with the beef, coconut milk, salt, lemongrass, bay leaves and kaffir lime leaves, if using. Bring to the boil, then reduce to a gentle simmer, stirring every 20 minutes to ensure the rendang doesn't stick to the base of the pan.

03　After 2–2½ hours, the oil from the coconut milk will split and rise to the surface, appearing as a reddish-orange oil – Indonesians call this stage 'kalio'. Depending on the oil content of your coconut milk, this may be a subtle film of oil or there can be a pool of it. Remove the lemongrass stalks – if they cook any further, they may disintegrate and be impossible to remove.

04　Turn the heat up to medium–high to reduce the sauce. Stir the rendang continuously until the sauce has thickened and turned a deep brown. As more oil separates, you are nearly there. Continue stirring the beef so it absorbs the sauce and caramelizes on the outside. Taste and adjust the seasoning if needed before serving.

VARIATION: TOFU AND BOILED EGG RENDANG

You can easily make a vegetarian rendang. Make the sauce following the steps in the recipe above, omitting the beef. Simmer the sauce and

YOU WILL ALSO NEED A FOOD PROCESSOR.

take it to the 'kalio' stage, where the oil separates. Reduce the sauce to your preferred consistency and then add six whole, peeled soft-boiled eggs and 300g (10½oz) of firm tofu, cut into cubes. Squeeze any excess moisture from the tofu using kitchen paper before adding it. Warm everything together, but don't try to caramelize the eggs or tofu or they will fall apart. Serve immediately.

VARIATION: RENDANG TOASTIES

If you have any leftover rendang and own a sandwich toaster, make rendang toasties. Using a basic sliced loaf, simply butter the outside of two slices of bread, turn them over and fill one side with the leftover rendang and some grated Cheddar. Make the sandwich and then toast until the toastie is golden on the outside. Serve with sambal.

BUL DAK

GF · ⏱ 35 MINS · SERVES 4 AS AN 'ANJU' (DRINKING SNACK) OR SIDE DISH · BY DA-HAE WEST

'Bul dak' literally translates as 'fire chicken', in Korean, due to the rich, spicy gochujang sauce. In Korea, bul dak is a popular 'anju' (food to soak up alcohol) as the tongue-tingling sauce is the perfect complement to a glass or few of soju or ice-cold beer. The cheese is often served melted and grilled on top of the chicken but it's even better when it is eaten bubbling hot with a river of oozy cheese around the edge to dip/wrap the chicken in. It is spicy, a little sweet and incredibly addictive!

GLUTEN-FREE: If you're cooking gluten-free, substitute the soy sauce for tamari and check the label of your mirin.

500G (1LB 2OZ) BONELESS SKINLESS
    CHICKEN THIGHS

3 SPRING ONIONS

3 TBSP VEGETABLE OIL

75G (2¾OZ) SLICED KOREAN RICE
    CAKES (OPTIONAL)

200G (7OZ) MOZZARELLA

100G (3½OZ) CHEDDAR CHEESE

FOR THE SAUCE:

3 GARLIC CLOVES

3 RED BIRDS EYE CHILLI

3 TBSP GOCHUGARU (KOREAN RED
    PEPPER FLAKES – SUBSTITUTE FOR
    CHILLI FLAKES IF YOU CAN'T FIND)

2 TBSP GOCHUJANG (KOREAN RED
    PEPPER PASTE)

2 TBSP KOREAN SOY SAUCE

2 TBSP MIRIN

1 TBSP HONEY

1 TBSP BROWN SUGAR

¼ TSP SESAME OIL

A PINCH OF SALT

01   Cut the chicken into bite-sized pieces and set aside. Finely chop the spring onions and set to one side.

02   To make the sauce, peel and mince the garlic cloves and finely chop the birds eye chillies. Add the chillies and garlic to a medium bowl along with the rest of the sauce ingredients and set to one side.

03   Pour the oil into a large frying pan over a medium heat. Add the chopped spring onions and cook for 2 minutes until they have softened.

04   Add the chicken and the sauce. Mix together and fry for 5 minutes – keep stirring to ensure the sauce does not catch.

05   If using rice cakes, add them to the pan and stir in. Continue to stir for a further 3–4 minutes until the rice cakes have softened and the chicken is cooked through.

06   In a separate frying pan, tear the mozzarella and assemble around the edge. Scatter the Cheddar on top of the mozzarella and make a well in the middle. Place over a medium heat and leave to melt.

07   Carefully spoon out the chicken (and rice cakes) from the first pan into the second pan so that the fiery chicken is surrounded by a river of cheese. Serve bubbling hot.

CHICKEN PASTILLA

DF · ⏱ 2 HRS 45 MINS · SERVES 4 SHAMELESS OR 6 POLITE GUESTS ·
BY SARIT PACKER & ITAMAR SRULOVICH, HONEY & CO

A traditional Moroccan pastilla is made with pigeon, scrambled eggs,
almonds and a light spicing of cinnamon – we have tried it several times
but it hasn't fully won us over. When we opened Honey & Co, we wanted
to recreate the best parts... the crispy, crunch in your mouth, pastry,
the braised soft spiced meat and the warm spicing. In our version, the
sweetness comes from dried fruit, the spicing is warm and comforting
and the chicken just works. You can prepare everything in advance and
simply bake just before serving for an easy, impressive dinner.

DAIRY-FREE: Use oil instead of
butter if cooking dairy-free.

6 CHICKEN THIGHS WITH SKIN AND
    BONES (APPROX. 800G/1LB 2OZ)
2 TSP SALT
1 TSP PEPPER
100G (3½OZ) PITTED DATES
3 ONIONS, SLICED THINLY (APPROX.
    300G/10½OZ)
1 CINNAMON STICK
1 DRIED RED CHILLI (YOU CAN REMOVE
    THE SEEDS IF YOU PREFER MILDER
    FLAVOURS)
2 TBSP RAS EL HANOUT SPICE MIX
240ML (8FL OZ) WATER
1 PACKET OF FILO PASTRY (APPROX.
    250–270G/9–9½OZ)
60G (2¼OZ) MELTED BUTTER (OR OIL)

01   Heat your oven to 200°C/180°C fan/gas mark 6.

02   Put a large frying pan over a medium heat. Place the chicken thighs skin-down in it and sprinkle with 1 teaspoon of the salt and the pepper. You won't need to add any oil to cook it in, as the skin will render a lot of fat – keep it on a medium heat and allow the skin to crisp and colour, this will take about 10–15 minutes. Once the skin is all crisp and golden, flip the thighs and cook on the other side for 5 minutes, then use tongs to remove them to an ovenproof pan that is large enough to contain them all in one layer. Add the pitted dates.

03   Keep the fat in the frying pan and add the sliced onions and the other teaspoon of salt. Cook the onions down until they are soft and starting to go golden. Add the cinnamon stick, dried chilli and ras el hanout and mix well. Cook for 30 seconds, then add the water and bring to the boil. Once boiling, pour over the chicken thighs in the ovenproof pan. Cover the pan and place in the centre of the oven to cook for 1 hour.

04   Open the lid carefully and check whether the chicken is fully cooked – it should just fall off the bone. If it is still a little tough, cook for a further 10–15 minutes. Set aside until cool enough to handle.

05   Carefully pour the contents of the pan into a sieve over a bowl. Retain the cooking liquid. Pull the chicken from the bones, discarding them along with any cartilage. Remove the chilli and the cinnamon stick. Mix the chicken meat together with the cooked dates and onions, along with just enough liquid so the mixture binds well – any remaining liquid can be kept to warm through and use as extra sauce when serving. You can prepare this chicken-date-onion mixture up to 2 days in advance. Store in the fridge until you are ready to assemble the pastilla.

06   Preheat your oven to 200°C/180°C fan/gas mark 6.

07   Lay the opened packet of filo pastry on the table. Carefully peel off the first sheet and use a brush to butter it, then fold into four and set aside (this folded square will give a thicker base to the pastilla). Peel off the next sheet and butter it, cover with another sheet and set aside. Repeat with two more sheets, so that you have two sheets of double thickness.

08   Place one doubled sheet lengthways on the table, put the folded square in the centre of it and lay the other doubled sheet on top at 90° to the first sheet, to make a cross-shape that is thickest in the middle.

09   Carefully lift the pastry cross off the table and place in a 22–24cm (8½-9½in) ovenproof frying pan or cake tin. Let it line the tin or pan with the sides of the pastry hanging over the edge. Fill with the chicken mixture and fold the corners over to cover it. We like to make the top a little crumpled so it looks natural. Brush the top of the pastry with the remaining butter and place in the centre of the oven for 15 minutes. After this time, turn the tin around so that the pastilla cooks evenly, and bake for a further 10–15 minutes or until the pastry is all golden and crisp.

10   Serve immediately, with a jug of the warm cooking liquid as sauce and a fresh green salad on the side.

BORANI KADOO

V, GF · ⏱ 2 HRS · SERVES 4 · BY MURSAL SAIQ, CUE POINT

A traditional Afghan dish with a Cue Point twist. Large chunks of roasted
or smoked pumpkin slowly braised in a flavourful combination of
aromatic spices, served with a spiced yoghurt to serve.

GLUTEN-FREE: If you're cooking gluten-free and serving with bread, choose a gluten-free alternative.

1 MEDIUM-SIZED PUMPKIN

1 ONION, PEELED

5 GARLIC CLOVES, PEELED

1 TSP CORIANDER SEEDS

1 TSP GROUND CUMIN

¼ TSP EACH OF GROUND GINGER,
   CHILLI FLAKES, SMOKED PAPRIKA,
   GROUND TURMERIC

2 TSP TOMATO PURÉE

8 LARGE TOMATOES

1 TBSP + ½ TSP VEGETABLE OIL

SEA SALT

SALT AND BLACK PEPPER

FOR THE AFGHAN YOGHURT

250G (9OZ) NATURAL YOGHURT (MAKE
   SURE TO START WITH A REALLY
   GOOD YOGHURT)

½ TSP DRIED MINT

ZEST OF ½ LEMON

1 SMALL GARLIC CLOVE, CRUSHED

¼ TSP GROUND CUMIN

¼ TSP CHILLI POWDER

FRESH NAAN BREAD OR RICE, TO SERVE
   → HEAD TO PAGE 117 FOR OUR
   HOMEMADE MOB NAAN RECIPE

01   Make the Afghan yoghurt. In a medium bowl, stir all the ingredients together to combine. Season to taste with salt and black pepper. Leave in the fridge until serving.

02   Preheat your oven to 180°C/160°C fan/gas mark 4 or if you have a smoker, light that.

03   Deseed the pumpkin, reserving the seeds, and slice into quarters, lightly oil all exposed sides and season with sea salt. Place on a baking tray, skin-side up, and cook in the oven or smoker for 45–55 minutes. (If smoking we recommend using oak for the smoker.) When the skin is lightly caramelized, remove from the oven or smoker. Wash the seeds, getting rid of all the pulp, and set aside to dry.

04   Make the tomato sauce. Dice the onions and thinly slice the garlic. Toast the coriander seeds in a small dry frying pan over a medium heat.

05   Get a large saucepan over a medium heat and drizzle in a good glug of oil. Add the onions and fry, stirring occasionally, until soft then stir in the garlic. Add the toasted coriander along with the ground spices and a good pinch of salt. Cook for 30 seconds then stir in the tomato purée. Roughly chop the tomatoes and tip them in too. Cook for 25 minutes, stirring occasionally, until the tomatoes have broken down. Season to taste with salt and black pepper.

06   Once the sauce has reduced, place the pumpkin into the pan. Let everything cook together on a low heat for 10–15 minutes until the pumpkin is soft and almost mushy in texture but still it still retains its shape.

07   Meanwhile, add the veg oil to a small frying pan over a medium heat. Lightly fry 4 tablespoons of the dried pumpkin seeds with a big pinch of salt and remove from the pan when their colour begins to change and they are nicely toasted.

08 Divide the borani kadoo between four bowls. Spoon over the Afghan yoghurt and garnish with toasted seeds. Serve with fresh naan breads or rice.

JOLLOF RICE

GF, DF · ⏱ 2 HRS · SERVES 4 · BY OYINDA ROBINSON

Oyinda's easy guide to an absolutely delicious homemade jollof rice,
Nigerian style. Fresh tomatoes and spicy infused rice. Go on MOB.

GLUTEN-FREE: Check the labels on your stocks if cooking gluten-free.

400G (14OZ) TIN OF CHOPPED
   TOMATOES OR 6 LARGE FRESH
   TOMATOES
1 RED PEPPER
2 MEDIUM ONIONS
1 TSP SMOKED PAPRIKA
110ML (3¾OZ) VEGETABLE OIL
75G (2¾OZ) TOMATO PURÉE
1 CHICKEN STOCK CUBE
1 MAGGI STOCK CUBE
4 BAY LEAVES
1 BUNCH OF FRESH THYME
1 SCOTCH BONNET
500G (1LB 2OZ) LONG GRAIN BASMATI
   RICE
SALT AND BLACK PEPPER

YOU WILL ALSO NEED A FOOD
PROCESSOR.

01   Blend the tomatoes, red pepper, one and a half onions and paprika together in a food processor. If using tinned tomatoes there is no need for water but if using whole tomatoes, add a splash of water.

02   Get a large saucepan over a medium heat. Drizzle in 2 tablespoons of the oil, chop up the other onion half and fry, stirring occasionally, until soft. Remove the onion and set aside.

03   Using the same pan, drizzle in the remaining oil and add your blended ingredients, as well as the thyme, both stock cubes, bay leaves (some whole and some torn up), the tomato purée and the whole scotch bonnet. Then, let this simmer until the oil begins to separate, around 15 minutes, while you prepare your rice.

04   Wash the rice to remove any starch, you will know the starch has washed away once the water runs clear.

05   Add the rice to the pan, and stir it in. Cover with 1 litre (1¾ pints) of boiling water. Bring it to a simmer and then let it putter away for 10 minutes or so until the liquid is absorbed and the rice is cooked through.

06   Season to taste with salt and black pepper. Then cover the saucepan and steam over a very low heat for 10 minutes.

07   Add your softened onions to the pan and mix them in. Cover and let it steam for a further 10 minutes. Serve at the table for everyone to tuck in!

VEGAN MAPO TOFU

VG, GF, DF · ⏱ 40 MINS · SERVES 4 · BY JULIAN DENIS OF MAO CHOW

Mapo tofu is the heart and soul of Sichuanese cuisine and is the perfect vehicle for punchy and bold Sichuanese flavours. It showcases the interplay between the spicy and numbing sensation known as 'mala' (which is one of the many flavour profiles of Sichuan). It also exempilfies joyous textural contrast between gentle doubanjiang slathered silken tofu and firm meaty mince. This recipe can be banged out on a weeknight with little effort and perhaps even when suffering from a hangover. Use this as a guide. There are no hard or fast rules when it comes to mapo tofu. Make it yours.

GLUTEN-FREE: Check the label of your doubanjiang and vegan mince if cooking gluten-free.

500G (1LB 2OZ) SILKEN TOFU

1 TBSP VEGETABLE OIL

2 TBSP FERMENTED BLACK BEANS, RINSED IN COLD WATER AND PATTED DRY

2 TSP CASTER SUGAR

2 TBSP DOUBANJIANG (ALSO CALLED TOBAN DIJAN)

200G (7OZ) VEGAN MINCE

2 TBSP CHILLI OIL

2 BUNCHES OF SPRING ONIONS, CUT INTO 2½CM (1IN) LONG PIECES

4 GARLIC CLOVES, PEELED AND FINELY GRATED

2 THUMB-SIZED PIECES OF FRESH GINGER, PEELED AND FINELY GRATED

1 TBSP SICHUAN PEPPERCORNS, TOASTED AND GROUND INTO POWDER

CORNFLOUR SLURRY (2 TBSP CORNFLOUR MIXED WITH 2 TBSP WATER)

STEAMED JASMINE RICE, TO SERVE

01 Gently cut the silken tofu into 2½cm (1in) cubes. Get a large saucepan of salted water (the water should be salty like the ocean) over a medium heat. Simmer the tofu on low for 10 minutes then carefully strain.

02 While the tofu is simmering, get a wok over a high heat and drizzle in the vegetable oil. Once the oil is hot, add the fermented black beans and sugar. Stir continuously until they become fragrant then lower the heat to medium.

03 Add the doubanjiang, stirring continuously so that the doubanjiang doesn't dry out and stick to the wok (add water to the mixture if it becomes too dry). Add the vegan mince and fry until slightly crisped.

04 Add 500ml (17fl oz) of water to the wok and then add your strained simmered silken tofu. Be very careful not to break the tofu cubes when incorporating into the other ingredients. At this point add your chilli oil, spring onions, garlic, ginger and 2 teaspoons of the Sichuan peppercorn powder. Mix gently.

05 Add the cornstarch slurry and gently incorporate. Simmer for a few minutes over a low heat and finish by sprinkling more Sichuan peppercorn powder on top. Serve with rice.

SPICY 'SHIN CUP' INSTANT RAMEN FRIED CHICKEN

⏱ 1 HR 15 MINS + OVERNIGHT MARINATING · SERVES 2 · BY CHICK 'N' SOURS

This is a very fun alternative way of using blitzed up dry instant noodles to coat fried chicken. Here we have used our favourite spicy instant noodle brand, Shin Cup Ramen. We have made our own version to use as a shake seasoning, in the brine and as the ramen soup base! The coating is super-crispy from the dry noodles and addictive from the spicy shake. We hope this recipe makes your hearts smile as much as ours. You will need a cooking thermometer for this.

2 CHICKEN SKIN-ON, BONE-IN LEGS, CUT INTO DRUMSTICKS AND THIGHS

4 PACKETS OF SHIN CUP SPICY INSTANT RAMEN

2 LITRES (3½ PINTS) VEGETABLE OIL

FOR THE SPICY SHAKE

50G (1¾OZ) CASTER SUGAR

4 TBSP HOT PAPRIKA

1 TBSP + 1TSP HOT SMOKED PAPRIKA

2 TBSP CAYENNE PEPPER

2 TSP FINE SALT

2 TSP GROUND CORIANDER

1½ TSP GROUND CUMIN

2 TSP MSG (OPTIONAL)

1 TBSP ONION POWDER

½ TSP DRIED OREGANO

1 1 TSP GARLIC POWDER

A BIG PINCH OF CITRIC ACID (OPTIONAL)

½ TSP GROUND BLACK PEPPER

FOR THE BRINE

2 TBSP OF SPICY SHAKE

500G (17FL OZ) BUTTERMILK

1TSP SALT

01 Measure all the ingredients for the spicy shake into a bowl and mix together. *The spice mix will keep in a jar for up to 6 months. Put it on everything.*

02 Add 2 tablespoons of the spicy shake into a separate bowl, measure in the buttermilk and salt then add the chicken pieces. Cover then brine the chicken in the fridge for at least 12 hours if not 24 hours.

03 Fried chicken time. Blitz the dried ramen noodle nests into a powder (we use a NutriBullet). Tip into a bowl – this is your flour. Whisk the egg and milk together for your wet mix.

04 Remove the chicken pieces from the buttermilk brine and shake off any excess buttermilk. Dredge the pieces of chicken into the noodle flour mix, then the wet batter, then back into the noodle flour, working it in with your hands.

05 Pour the oil into a deep saucepan and heat until 140°C/285°F. Fry the chicken for 7–8 mins until it starts to turn golden brown remove and set aside.

06 Increase the temperature to 160°C/320°F. Fry for the second time for around 4–5 minutes until the chicken is cooked through. Season liberally all over both sides with the spicy shake.

07 For the spicy ramen broth, cook two of the ramen soup sachets with water according to the packet instructions.

FOR THE WET MIX
1 LARGE EGG
120ML (4FL OZ) WHOLE MILK

08 To serve ladle the spicy ramen broth into two Asian-style soup bowls. Place the fried chicken on a large plate and serve with pickles on the side and a bowl of the spicy ramen broth.

7

PUDDINGS

Puds that will warm you
to your core.

MISO STICKY TOFFEE PUDDING

V · ⏱ 1 HR 40 MINS + PLUS COOLING · MAKES 1 LOAF – SERVES 6–8

Not your average sticky toffee pudding. Using a technique inspired by St. John – one of London's finest restaurants – the sponge in this recipe is baked in a loaf tin, then sliced and reheated before being covered in a sweet and savoury miso sauce. The result is an excellent sauce-to-pud ratio which, let's be honest, is what everyone wants from a sticky toffee pudding.

BUDGET HACK: Skip the miso in the sauce. It will be classic and still banging.

250G (9OZ) SOFT BUTTER, PLUS EXTRA
    FOR GREASING

350G (12OZ) SOFT BROWN SUGAR

2 LARGE EGGS

2 TBSP BLACK TREACLE

200G (7OZ) SELF-RAISING FLOUR

2 PINCHES OF SALT

200G (7OZ) PITTED DATES

1 TSP BICARBONATE OF SODA

2–3 TBSP WHITE MISO

300ML (10½FL OZ) DOUBLE CREAM

ICE CREAM, TO SERVE

01   Preheat your oven to 180°C/160°C fan/gas mark 4. Use a little butter to grease a 2lb/900g loaf tin. Line the base with baking paper.

02   Blitz 75g (2¾oz) of butter and 175g (6oz) of brown sugar together in a food processor. Add the eggs, treacle and flour along with a pinch of salt. Blitz again to form a thick cake batter, then scrape into a large bowl.

03   Put the dates into the food processor (no need to clean first) and add the bicarb. Pour in 300ml (10½fl oz) of boiling water and blitz to a purée. Pour the date purée into the cake batter and whisk well to combine. Pour into your loaf tin and bake for 45–50 minutes until well risen and a skewer or knife inserted into the centre comes out with a few dry crumbs attached. Leave to cool then remove from its tin. *The pudding is even better made the day before and left well wrapped.*

04   Sauce time. Put the remaining 175g (6oz) of butter, 175g (6oz) of sugar, 2 tablespoons of miso, double cream and a pinch of salt into a saucepan. Cook over a medium heat, stirring occasionally, until the butter and sugar have melted and you are left with a glossy toffee sauce. Bring to the boil and bubble away for 10 minutes to thicken slightly. Taste, adding more miso if you like.

05   Slice the loaf into portions and transfer to a foil-lined baking tray. Spoon plenty of sauce over each slice, then cover with foil. Reheat in the oven for 10 minutes until warmed through. Transfer the warm pudding into bowls and serve with ice cream and more sauce.

COOKIE DOUGH PIE

V · ⏱ 1 HOUR PLUS CHILLING · SERVES 8–10

We've got our friend Bella to thank for this ridiculous creation as it's something that she used to eat at her mate's house when she was a kid. A flaky layer of homemade pastry slathered in Nutella and topped with hazelnut cookie dough. So good.

BUDGET HACK: Leave out the hazelnuts.

380G (13½OZ) PLAIN FLOUR

220G (7¾OZ) COLD BUTTER

75G (2¾OZ) CASTER SUGAR, PLUS 1 TBSP

A PINCH OF SALT

50G (1¾OZ) BLANCHED HAZELNUTS (OPTIONAL)

75G (2¾OZ) SOFT BROWN SUGAR

1 LARGE EGG

1 TSP VANILLA EXTRACT

1 TSP BAKING POWDER

100G (3½OZ) MILK OR DARK CHOCOLATE

5 TBSP NUTELLA

ICE CREAM, TO SERVE

01 Pastry time. Measure 200g (7oz) of the flour into a bowl or food processor. Cut 100g (3½oz) of the cold butter into small cubes. Add to the flour then either blitz or rub together using your fingertips until breadcrumbs form. Mix in 1 tablespoon of caster sugar and a pinch of salt then pour in 2 tablespoons of cold water. Blitz or beat until it just comes together, if it looks a little dry add 1 more tablespoon of water. Tip the pastry out onto your work surface and briefly knead until smooth. Cover and chill in the fridge for 30 minutes.

02 Meanwhile, make your cookie dough. Toast the hazelnuts, if using, then leave to cool. Soften (don't melt) the remaining 120g (4¼oz) of butter in the microwave. In a large mixing bowl beat it with both the sugars until creamy. Crack in the egg, add the vanilla extract and mix to combine. Tip in the remaining 180g (6½oz) of flour, baking powder and a pinch of salt. Beat to form a cookie dough. Roughly chop up the chocolate and hazelnuts, then mix through the dough.

03 Preheat your oven to 180°C/160°C fan/gas mark 4.

04 Get your pastry out of the fridge. Flour your surface. Roll out the pastry to roughly 1cm (½in) thickness and line a 20cm (8in) tart tin. Press the pastry into the edges of the tin. Cut off any excess pastry and patch up any holes, if you have any.

05 Spoon the Nutella all over the base of the pastry, then use the back of your spoon to roughly spread. Don't worry about it being a super-even layer as you don't want to break the pastry.

06 Spoon the cookie dough over the Nutella layer. Bake in the oven for 35 minutes until the top is golden brown, the edges are set and the middle still a little wobbly.

07 Serve warm with ice-cream or cooled with a cup of tea.

CHOCOLATE JAFFA POOL

V · ○ 50 MINS · SERVES 4

This magic pudding defies logic, MOB. It's like the Derren Brown of desserts. You pour a hot chocolate sauce all over a sponge, pop it in the oven for about half an hour, and out comes this gloriously-risen cake that sits in a pool of gooey chocolatey sauce. We've even added chunks of orange chocolate for extra indulgence. You're welcome.

BUDGET HACK: This one is good as it is.

75G (2¾OZ) BUTTER, PLUS EXTRA FOR GREASING

100G (3½OZ) ORANGE CHOCOLATE → USE A DARK CHOCOLATE ORANGE OR GO FOR TERRY'S IF YOU FANCY EXTRA COMFORT

170G (6OZ) SELF-RAISING FLOUR

200G (7OZ) SOFT BROWN SUGAR

50G (1¾OZ) COCOA POWDER

A LARGE PINCH OF SALT

100ML (3½FL OZ) WHOLE MILK

2 LARGE EGGS

1 ORANGE

ICE CREAM OR CREAM, TO SERVE

01   Preheat your oven to 180°C/160°C fan/gas mark 4. Grease the bottom of a smallish baking dish with butter.

02   Snap 50g (1¾oz) of the chocolate into a microwaveable bowl and add the butter. Blast in the microwave on high for 30 seconds at a time, then stir until the chocolate has completely melted. (Don't cook the chocolate for longer than 30 seconds in one go as it can burn.) Roughly chop the remaining chocolate and set both aside.

03   Measure the flour, 100g (3½oz) of the sugar and 30g (1 oz) of the cocoa powder into a large mixing bowl and add a big pinch of salt. Pour the milk into a jug, crack in the eggs and the zest and juice of the orange. Whisk to combine.

04   Pour the wet ingredients, along with the melted butter and chocolate, into the dry ingredients. Whisk together until smooth then stir in the chocolate chunks. Scrape the batter into your baking dish and smooth out the top.

05   Boil the kettle. Measure the remaining 100g (3½oz) of sugar and 20g (¾oz) of cocoa powder into a medium bowl. Pour in 250ml (9fl oz) of boiling water and whisk together with a fork until all the sugar has dissolved. Pour the chocolate sauce all over the cake batter (don't worry it will look a bit weird at this point).

06   Carefully transfer to the oven. Bake for 25–30 minutes until the sponge is well risen and firm to the touch – all that chocolate sauce will have seeped underneath. Serve warm with ice cream or cream. *Reheat in the microwave to keep things moist.*

PBJ ROLLS

V · ⏱ 35 MINS · MAKES 10 ROLLS

This one's a moreish mash up: a cheat's take on a Scandi bun,
made using puff pastry, that's filled with our favourite PB&J combo.
So easy and so, so tasty. You'll be making these every week,
much to everyone's delight.

BUDGET HACK: This one is good as is.

30G (1OZ) BUTTER

75G (2½OZ) SMOOTH PEANUT BUTTER

5 TBSP RASPBERRY JAM

1 PACKET OF READY-ROLLED PUFF PASTRY

1 EGG, BEATEN

1 TBSP DEMERARA SUGAR

YOU WILL ALSO NEED BAKING PAPER.

01   Preheat your oven to 200°C/180°C fan/gas mark 6. Line a large baking tray with baking paper.

02   Melt the butter in a small bowl, add the peanut butter and mix together. Put the jam into a separate bowl and give it a good stir to loosen.

03   Unravel the sheet of puff pastry so that one of the longer edges is towards you. Spread the peanut butter all over the sheet of pastry followed by the jam. Roll the pastry away from you into a long sausage then cut into 10 rolls.

04   Place the rolls with the swirl facing up onto your baking tray, leaving 2–3cm (1in) between each one so they have room to spread. Using your hands, squash down the rolls halfway as this will encourage the swirl to stay. Brush the rolls with the egg wash, then sprinkle over the sugar. Bake in the oven for 20 minutes until cooked through. Don't worry, they may unravel slightly but they'll be delicious.

05   Serve warm or cold, preferably with a coffee. These will keep in an airtight container for 3 days.

ULTIMATE BROWNIE

V · ⏱ 45 MINS · MAKES 12 SQUARES

Proudly presenting: our ultimate brownie recipe. We've looked at
all the credentials for what makes the best brownie and combined them
in this one glorious recipe. Crackly top. Gooey, squidgy centre.
Crustier ends. Pools of chopped up chocolate. Go on.

BUDGET HACK: Use
supermarket own brand
chocolate.

200G (7OZ) DARK CHOCOLATE
250G (9OZ) BUTTER
2 LARGE PINCHES OF SALT
100G (3½OZ) MILK CHOCOLATE
300G (10½OZ) CASTER SUGAR
3 LARGE EGGS
60G (2¼OZ) SELF-RAISING FLOUR
60G (2¼OZ) COCOA POWDER

YOU WILL ALSO NEED BAKING PAPER.

01   Preheat your oven to 180°C/160°C fan/gas mark 4. Grease a 20cm
(8in) brownie tin or high-sided roasting tray with butter and line the base
with baking paper.

02   Snap the dark chocolate into a microwaveable bowl, add the butter
and a big pinch of salt. Zap in the microwave on high in 30-second
bursts, stirring in between, until the butter and chocolate are completely
melted. Set aside to cool slightly. Roughly chop the milk chocolate.

03   Measure the sugar into a large bowl. Crack in the eggs. Using an
electric whisk, whisk the eggs and sugar together until they have almost
doubled in size and are very light and fluffy.

04   Pour in the melted chocolate mixture and add the flour and cocoa
powder. Whisk briefly until everything is combined.

05   Smooth half the brownie batter into your tin. Scatter over half the
milk chocolate then scrape the rest of the batter over the top. Sprinkle
over the remaining milk chocolate and a big pinch of sea salt. Bake for 30
minutes or until the edges are set and the centre still has a good wobble.

06   Leave to cool then cut into 12 squares.

CLASSIC BREAD & BUTTER PUDDING

V · ⏱ 55 MINS · SERVES 4

Some things are better off left untouched, and this is one of them. It's bread and butter pudding as it should be done: thick-sliced white bread, lashings of custard, plump sultanas, and a crunchy sugar top. Simple.

BUDGET HACK: Use 100g (3½oz) of sultanas and the zest of 1 lemon instead of the mixed peel.

9 SLICES OF WHITE BREAD
50G (1¾OZ) SOFT BUTTER
75G (2¾OZ) SULTANAS
50G (1¾OZ) MIXED PEEL
3 LARGE EGGS
300ML (10½FL OZ) WHOLE MILK
150ML (5FL OZ) DOUBLE CREAM
1 TSP VANILLA EXTRACT
A PINCH OF SALT
3 TBSP DEMERARA SUGAR

01   Preheat the oven to 180°C/160°C fan/gas mark 4. Get out a medium-sized baking dish.

02   Cut the crusts off the bread and spread each slice on one side with butter then cut into triangles. Lay half of the bread buttered-side down into the baking dish. Scatter over half of the sultanas and all of the mixed peel. Lay the remaining bread, buttered-side down, on top (you may need to overlap it slightly). Sprinkle over the remaining sultanas.

03   Crack the eggs into a large bowl. Pour in the milk and cream. Add the vanilla extract and a pinch of salt and whisk to form a smooth custard. Pour the custard over the prepared bread slices, pressing down on the bread so that it gets a proper soak.

04   Sprinkle the sugar evenly over the top. Bake in the oven for 35–40 minutes until the top is golden brown and the pudding has puffed up slightly. Leave to rest for 5 minutes before serving at the table for everyone to help themselves and tuck in.

ALMOND PRALINE RICE PUDDING

GF, V · ⏱ 45 MINS · SERVES 4

Rice pudding is the ultimate comfort pud, rich and creamy with
unctuously soft rice. We've taken it up a notch by adding the crispiest,
crunchy, caramelized nutty praline. It's heaven in a bowl.

BUDGET HACK: Leave out the
booze.

1 VANILLA POD
200G (7OZ) PUDDING RICE
1 LITRE (1¾ PINTS) WHOLE MILK
150G (5½OZ) CASTER SUGAR
50G (1¾OZ) BLANCHED ALMONDS
SEA SALT
150ML (5 FL OZ) DOUBLE CREAM
A SLOSH OF BOOZE → BRANDY, WHISKY
    OR RUM (OPTIONAL)

01   Scrape the seeds out of the vanilla pod and add both to a medium-sized saucepan. Measure in the rice, milk and 50g (1¾oz) of caster sugar along with a pinch of salt. Cook over a medium heat, stirring often so that it doesn't catch, for around 35 minutes until the rice is cooked and creamy with a little bite.

02   Meanwhile, make the almond brittle. Line a small baking tray with baking paper.

03   Toast the almonds in a small, dry frying pan over a medium heat until lightly golden and smelling nutty. Tip out onto the baking paper and arrange in an even layer.

04   Put the frying pan back over the heat, sprinkle in the remaining 100g of caster sugar. Leave to caramelize, swirling the pan occasionally so the sugar melts evenly – do not stir. Once a deep amber colour, carefully pour the caramel over the almonds. Sprinkle over some sea salt and leave to cool. Almond brittle done!

05   Come back to the rice pudding. Once cooked, stir through the double cream and a good slosh of booze, if using. Keep warm.

06   Pulse the brittle in a mini food processor until you have a few smaller and larger pieces.

07   Diving the rice pudding between four bowls, top with the brittle and enjoy!

HONEYCOMB PROFITEROLES

V · ⏱ 1 HR 30 MINS · SERVES 4

Profiteroles are up there in the top tier of puddings. It might seem complicated, but making your own choux pastry is very forgiving. Just make sure to let it cool enough before you add the eggs. We've added honeycomb to the cream and topped with a classic chocolate sauce.

BUDGET HACK: Leave out the honeycomb and go classic with your profiteroles, adding 2 tablespoons of icing sugar to the cream instead.

75G (2¾OZ) BUTTER
100G (3½OZ) PLAIN FLOUR
2 PINCHES OF SALT
2 LARGE EGGS → MOB IT'S SUPER
    IMPORTANT YOU USE LARGE
    EGGS TO GET THE FLUFFIEST
    PROFITEROLES
600ML (21FL OZ) DOUBLE CREAM
4 CRUNCHIES (OR OTHER CHOCOLATE-
    COVERED HONEYCOMB)
100G (3½OZ) CASTER SUGAR
50G (1¾OZ) COCOA POWDER

YOU WILL ALSO NEED A ROLLING PIN.

01   Preheat your oven to 200°C/180°C fan/gas mark 6.

02   Cut the butter into small cubes. Chuck into a medium saucepan and pour in 200ml (7fl oz) of water. Put the pan over a low heat – you want to melt the butter without evaporating any of the water.

03   Meanwhile, measure the flour into a bowl and add a pinch of salt.

04   Come back to your saucepan. Once all the butter has melted, bring to the boil. Take off the heat, quickly tip in all of the flour and beat well with a wooden spoon to create a dough. Leave to cool for 4–5 minutes until just warm to the touch. While the mixture is cooling, crack the eggs into a jug and whisk well to combine.

05   Beat the eggs into the dough, bit by bit – make sure all of the egg is incorporated before you add the next bit. Once all the egg has been added you will be left with a thick glossy mixture.

06   Onto two baking trays spoon heaped teaspoons of the mixture, leaving a nice gap between each one so they have room to spread. Bake in the oven for 20–25 minutes until the profiteroles are puffed up, crisp and deeply golden. You will know when they are done because they will come away from the tray easily.

07   Once cooked, turn the profiteroles upside down. Using the end of a teaspoon, create a hole in the bottom of each one – this is for the filling. Return to the oven upside down for 5 minutes to let the insides dry out. Remove and leave to cool on a wire rack.

08   Filling time. Whisk the double cream in a medium bowl until it is just holding its shape. Bash up two of the Crunchies into small pieces using a rolling pin and fold through the whipped cream. Using a teaspoon, fill the cooled profiteroles with the cream. Pile onto a sharing plate.

09   Chocolate sauce time. Measure 100ml (3½fl oz) of water into a small saucepan over a medium heat. Add the caster sugar and bring to a simmer – you just want the sugar to dissolve then whisk in the cocoa powder along with a pinch of salt.

10   Drizzle the sauce over the profiteroles. Smash up the remaining Crunchies with your rolling pin and scatter over the top. The dream pudding.

CARAMELIZED APPLE PUDDING

V · ⏲ 1 HR · SERVES 4

This recipe is inspired by Soph's grandma, who only really eats sweet things and considers the humble apple sponge to be the most comforting pud in the world. We've taken it up a notch by making our own apple caramel from scratch. Do Grandma proud by eating it straight from the dish while it's still warm.

BUDGET HACK: Don't bother with the vanilla in the sponge, it will still be delicious.

220G (7¾OZ) CASTER SUGAR
150G (5½OZ) SOFT BUTTER
100ML (3½FL OZ) APPLE JUICE
A PINCH OF SALT
2 LARGE BRAMLEY APPLES
2 LARGE EGGS
1 TSP VANILLA EXTRACT
120G (4¼OZ) SELF-RAISING FLOUR
1 TBSP WHOLE MILK
CUSTARD OR ICE CREAM, TO SERVE

01   Preheat your oven to 180°C/160°C fan/gas mark 4.

02   Measure 100g (3½oz) of the caster sugar into a small saucepan then add 2 tablespoons of water. Put over a low heat and do not stir. Leave the sugar to melt and then caramelize, swirling the pan occasionally, for 8–10 minutes. Once amber in colour, carefully whisk in 30g (1oz) of the butter and the apple juice to make your apple caramel (it will splutter slightly and clump, but don't worry as it will become smooth again). Season with a big pinch of salt. Take off the heat and leave to cool slightly.

03   Peel, core and thickly slice the apples. Place, overlapping, in the bottom of a medium baking dish. Pour over the caramel.

04   Sponge time. With a wooden spoon, beat the remaining butter and caster sugar together in a medium bowl until creamy. Crack in the eggs, add the vanilla and mix well to combine. Tip in the flour, then stir to create a smooth batter, pouring in the milk to loosen.

05   Dollop the sponge batter on top of the apples, smoothing out the top. Bake in the oven for 30 minutes until the sponge is golden and just cooked through. Dish-up warm with custard or ice cream. *You can make this in advance and reheat in the oven or microwave.*

BOOZY BANOFFEE

V · ⏱ 30 MINS + AT LEAST 2 HRS CHILLING · MAKES 1 PIE · SERVES 6–8

You can't beat a classic banoffee pie when it's made with a buttery
biscuit base, homemade dulce de leche, bananas and airy
whipped cream. Well, you can a bit actually if you add a dash of
rum and top it all off with a chocolate flake.

BUDGET HACK: Go for an austerity pie and take out the booze and the flake.

250G (9OZ) DIGESTIVE BISCUITS
200G (7OZ) BUTTER
50G (1¾OZ) SOFT BROWN SUGAR
397G (14OZ) TIN OF CONDENSED MILK
A LARGE PINCH OF SALT
300ML (10½FL OZ) DOUBLE CREAM
3 TBSP RUM (WE LIKE A SPICED RUM)
1 TBSP ICING SUGAR
2 JUST RIPE BANANAS
1 SMALL FLAKE

YOU WILL ALSO NEED A ROLLING PIN
OR FOOD PROCESSOR.

01   Crush the biscuits with a rolling pin or food processor until they resemble fine breadcrumbs. Melt 125g (4½oz) of the butter in the microwave or in a small saucepan over a medium heat. Pour into a bowl and mix to combine. Get a 20cm (8in) springform tin and flip the base upside down as this will help you get the pie out more easily). Tip the buttery biscuits into the tin and use your fingers to press them up the sides of the tin to create your banoffee pie shell. Chill in the fridge.

02   Meanwhile, make your dulce de leche. Measure the remaining 50g (1¾oz) of butter and the sugar into a medium saucepan. Put over a low heat and leave to melt, stirring occasionally. Once fully incorporated pour in the condensed milk. Bring to the boil and cook, stirring constantly for 2–3 minutes, until the mixture has become lightly caramel-coloured. You need to stir the whole time so it doesn't catch (using a spatula here is easiest if you have one). Season with a big pinch of salt.

03   Get the biscuit base out of the fridge and pour your hot dulce de leche over it. Put it back in the fridge for at least 1 hour until set. *You can do this the night before.*

04   Once set, pour your double cream into a large bowl along with the rum. Add the icing sugar, then whisk until the boozy cream just holds its shape.

05   Get the tart out of the fridge. Slice the bananas and arrange on top of the caramel, then spoon over the whipped cream. Crush the flake over the top with your hands to serve. This will keep in fridge for 2–3 days.

CRUMBLE

V · ⏱ 1 HR · EACH SERVES 4

We know that everyone loves a crumble, but we also know that
you're going to love this particular crumble more than any other. In fact,
we're so confident that we've perfected the buttery, biscuit topping
that we've given you not one but two fillings to enjoy. Go classic
with cinnamon-spiced apple and blackberry or enjoy the soothing
warmth of stem ginger and rhubarb.

BUDGET HACK: Use frozen
berries in the apple crumble
instead.

TOPPING
120G (4½OZ) COLD BUTTER, PLUS
    EXTRA FOR GREASING
180G (6½OZ) PLAIN FLOUR
60G (2¼OZ) SOFT BROWN SUGAR
A PINCH OF SALT

FOR THE APPLE & BLACKBERRY
2 LARGE BRAMLEY APPLES
150G (5½OZ) BLACKBERRIES
1 TBSP SOFT BROWN SUGAR
1 TSP GROUND CINNAMON

FOR THE RHUBARB & GINGER
400G (14OZ) RHUBARB
3 BALLS OF STEM GINGER, PLUS 2 TBSP
    OF SYRUP
1 ORANGE

ICE CREAM, CUSTARD, CREAM OR
    YOGHURT, TO SERVE

01   Preheat your oven to 200°C/180°C fan/gas mark 6. Grease a
medium baking dish with a bit of butter.

02   Crumble topping time. Cut the butter into rough cubes. Measure
the flour into a large bowl. Tip in the butter then use your fingertips to
rub the two together, until the mixture looks like big sandy-coloured
breadcrumbs. Stir in the brown sugar and a pinch of salt, squashing any
sugar lumps with your fingers. Set aside.

03   *For the apple and blackberry filling:* peel, core and thickly slice the
apples. Layer into the baking dish along with the blackberries. Sprinkle
over the sugar and cinnamon. *For the rhubarb filling:* cut the rhubarb
into 2½cm (1in)-long long pieces and roughly chop the stem ginger. Mix
together in a bowl along with the stem ginger syrup and the zest and
juice of the orange. Pile into the baking dish (no need to be neat, it will
collapse once cooked).

04   Come back to your topping. Use your hands to pile it on top of the
fruit, scrunching some bits of the topping as you go to form some nice
clusters (these will go extra crisp). Bake the crumble for 25–30 minutes
(apple) or 35–40 minutes (rhubarb) until bubbling and golden. Dish up
with dairy of your choice. We love eating it with our Proper Custard on
page 249.

PROPER CUSTARD

V, GF · ⏱ 15 MINS · SERVES 4

You can't have a book on comfort food and not include a
recipe for vanilla custard. Once you've tried our fool-proof method,
and realize how easy it is to make, you'll never go back to
the shop-bought stuff ever again.

BUDGET HACK: Use 1 teaspoon
of vanilla extract instead.

1 VANILLA POD
500ML (17FL OZ) WHOLE MILK
3 LARGE EGG YOLKS → FREEZE THE EGG
    WHITES TO MAKE A PAVLOVA
2 TBSP CORNFLOUR
3 TBSP CASTER SUGAR

01   Cut the vanilla pod in half lengthways then use a cutlery knife to
scrape out the seeds. Add the seeds to a bowl and put the used pod into
a medium saucepan.

02   Pour the milk into the saucepan. Set over a medium heat and bring
to a simmer.

03   Meanwhile, whisk the egg yolks, vanilla seeds, cornflour and caster
sugar into a paste.

04   Once the milk is visibly steaming take it off the heat. Gradually pour
the warmed milk into the egg mixture in batches, whisking continuously.
Wait until the first lot has been incorporated into the mixture before you
add the next. Once all the milk has been poured in, return the whole lot
to the pan (no need to clean it first).

05   Place a sieve over a jug. Put the saucepan back on a medium heat
and cook, stirring constantly, until the custard has thickened, this will
only take a couple of minutes. Pour the custard through the sieve into
the jug to get rid of any lumps. *You can rinse the vanilla pod, dry it and
then keep in a bag of caster sugar for your own vanilla sugar.*

06   Serve the custard straight away or put a piece of cling film directly
on top of the custard to be reheated later (the cling film will stop a skin
from forming).

Index

Acknowledgements

First and foremost, I would like to thank the genius that is Sophie Godwin, who was behind most of the recipes in this book. Sophie, you are brilliant – your ideas are so creative and incredible, time and time again. I am so grateful that you are part of the MOB – our books are so much better because of it.

It was important to Sophie and myself that the recipes from the Around The World chapter came from chefs and contributor's that had grown up around those cuisines. So I would also like to thank all of our guest contributors for the recipes. You have all enriched this book immeasurably, and I know the MOB will love and use your creations time and time again.

In relation to *Comfort MOB*, I would like to thank the maestro that is David Loftus. You are a master of your art. And I will always be so grateful for the way you took us all in to your home during such a tough period. And thank you Ange for being there for us all.

On to the styling – Ellie Silcock, the most talent, hardworking food stylist there is. I have never enjoyed working side-by-side with someone in the kitchen as much as I do with you. It was a really special shoot, and that was so much down to your calming, steadying presence. You brought the recipes to life and the food looks so delicious, because of you.

And I am very grateful to our brilliant food assistant Sonali Shah; the shoots were so much easier with you at our side. Huge thanks to Adam Bush too, for writing all the incredible bread recipes.

Thank you also to Charlie Phillips for the best props and to OMSE for the designs!

Last but not least, I would like to thank the whole Hodder team. I am so thrilled to be part of the wider Hachette family. Carolyn, thank you for being so supportive throughout the process, and for seeing and understanding the vision. Issy, thank you for being so wonderful and for keeping everything on track. I feel sure the whole thing would be about four months delayed without you.

Next up, behind this book and every project we put out, there is the wonderful, the amazing MOB Kitchen team: Michael, Alice, Olivia, Morgan, Toby, T'yanna, Meg, Sophie KT, Sophie W, Seema and Lucas. This has been a huge project and it wouldn't have been possible without the incredible team we have running the business. I am also very grateful to Joe Glick for your support. I would like to give a quick special thanks to Lucas, your writing flair has made the difference with this book.

Finally, on to some personal thanks. My family have been the most constant source of encouragement and support since MOB Kitchen began. My mum, dad, and my brothers Joe and Sam. Joe – thank you for all your help with the design, I can't tell you how much it meant to me. Also, thank you to my wonderful girlfriend Robyn. You are the rock by my side always. I love you.

I want to mention my two grandparents, Pompa and Grandma, who both passed away during the production of this book. They were taken by Coronavirus, and I want to just say that I love you both and you will forever be in my heart.

Ben x

First published in Great Britain in 2021 by
Hodder & Stoughton
An Hachette UK company

1

Copyright © Hodder & Stoughton Ltd 2021
Recipes copyright © Mob Kitchen Ltd.
Photography copyright © David Loftus

SPICY 'SHIN CUP' INSTANT RAMEN FRIED CHICKEN
Adapted from *The Whole Chicken* © Carl Clarke
(London: Hardie Grant UK, 2020);
RENDANG DAGING Taken from *Coconut and Sambal* ©
Lara Lee (Bloomsbury Publishing, 2020);
CHICKEN PASTILLA Taken from *Honey & Co: Food
From the Middle East* © Sarit Packer & Itamar Srulovich
(London: Headline Home, 2014)

A CIP catalogue record for this title is available from
the British Library

Hardback 978 1 529 36981 6
eBook 978 1 529 36982 3

Editorial Director: Carolyn Thorne
Project Editor: Isabel Gonzalez-Prendergast
Copy Editor: Grace Paul
Design direction: OMSE
Layout design: Nicky Barneby
Photography: David Loftus
Food Stylist: Elena Silcock
Props Stylist: Charlie Phillips
Production Manager: Claudette Morris

Colour origination by Alta London
Printed and bound in Germany by Mohn Media GmbH

Hodder & Stoughton policy is to use papers that are
natural, renewable and recyclable products and made
from wood grown in sustainable forests. The logging and
manufacturing processes are expected to conform to the
environmental regulations of the country of origin.

Hodder & Stoughton Ltd
Carmelite House
50 Victoria Embankment
London
EC4Y 0DZ

www.hodder.co.uk